DEFINING MOMENTS
WATERGATE

DEFINING MOMENTS
WATERGATE

Kevin Hillstrom

Omnigraphics

615 Griswold, Detroit MI 48226

Omnigraphics, Inc.

Kevin Hillstrom, *Series Editor*
Cherie D. Abbey, *Managing Editor*
Barry Puckett, *Research Associate*
Liz Barbour, *Permissions Associate*

Matthew P. Barbour, *Senior Vice President*
Kay Gill, *Vice President – Directories*
Kevin Hayes, *Operations Manager*
Leif A. Gruenberg, *Development Manager*
David P. Bianco, *Marketing Director*

Peter E. Ruffner, *Publisher*
Frederick G. Ruffner, *Chairman*

Copyright © 2004 Omnigraphics, Inc.
ISBN 0-7808-0769-3

Library of Congress Cataloging-in-Publication Data

Watergate / edited by Kevin Hillstrom.
  p. cm. -- (Defining moments)
  Includes bibliographical references (p.   ) and index.
  ISBN 0-7808-0769-3 (acid-free paper)
 1. Watergate Affair (1972-1974) I. Hillstrom, Kevin, 1963- II. Series.
  E860.W335 2004
  973.924--dc22

                                                                              2004015995

The information in this publication was compiled from the sources cited and from other sources considered reliable. Additional copyright information can be found on the photograph credits page of this book. While every possible effort has been made to ensure reliability, the publisher will not assume liability for damages caused by inaccuracies in the data, and makes no warranty, express or implied, on the accuracy of the information contained herein.

∞

This book is printed on acid-free paper meeting the ANSI Z39.48 Standard. The infinity symbol that appears above indicates that the paper in this book meets that standard.

Printed in the United States

TABLE OF CONTENTS

NARRATIVE OVERVIEW

BIOGRAPHIES

PRIMARY SOURCES

PREFACE

Throughout the course of America's existence, its people, culture, and institutions have been periodically challenged—and in many cases transformed—by profound historical events. Some of these momentous events, such as women's suffrage, the civil rights movement, and U.S. involvement in World War II, invigorated the nation and strengthened American confidence and capabilities. Others, such as the McCarthy era, the Vietnam War, and Watergate, have prompted troubled assessments and heated debates about the country's core beliefs and character.

Some of these defining moments in American history were years or even decades in the making. The Harlem Renaissance and the New Deal, for example, unfurled over the span of several years, while the American labor movement and the Cold War evolved over the course of decades. Other defining moments, such as the Cuban missile crisis and the terrorist attacks of September 11, 2001, transpired over a matter of days or weeks.

But although significant differences exist among these events in terms of their duration and their place in the timeline of American history, all share the same basic characteristic: they transformed the United States' political, cultural, and social landscape for future generations of Americans.

Taking heed of this fundamental reality, American citizens, schools, and other institutions are increasingly emphasizing the importance of understanding our nation's history. Omnigraphics' new *Defining Moments* series was created for the express purpose of meeting this growing appetite for authoritative, useful historical resources. This new series, which focuses on the most pivotal events in U.S. history from the 20th century forward, will be of enduring value to anyone interested in learning more about America's past—and in understanding how those historical events continue to reverberate in the 21st century.

Each individual volume of *Defining Moments* provides a valuable resource for readers interested in learning about the most profound events in our nation's history. Each volume is organized into three distinct sections— Narrative Overview, Biographies, and Primary Sources.

- The **Narrative Overview** provides readers with a detailed, factual account of the origins and progression of the "defining moment" being examined. It also explores the event's lasting impact on America's political and cultural landscape.

- The **Biographies** section provides valuable biographical background on leading figures associated with the event in question. Each biography concludes with a list of sources for further information on the profiled individual.

- The **Primary Sources** section collects a wide variety of pertinent primary source materials from the era under discussion, including official documents, papers and resolutions, letters, oral histories, memoirs, editorials, and other important works.

Individually, each of these sections is a rich resource for users. Together, they comprise an authoritative, balanced, and absorbing examination of some of the most significant events in U.S. history.

Other notable features contained within each volume in the series include a glossary of important individuals, places, and terms; a detailed chronology featuring page references to relevant sections of the narrative; an annotated bibliography of sources for further study; an extensive general bibliography that reflects the wide range of historical sources consulted by the author; and a subject index.

Acknowledgements

This series was developed in consultation with a distinguished Advisory Board comprised of public librarians, school librarians, and educators. They evaluated the series as it developed, and their comments and suggestions were invaluable throughout the production process. Any errors in this and other volumes in the series are ours alone. Following is a list of board members who contributed to the *Defining Moments* series:

Gail Beaver, M.A., M.A.L.S.
Adjunct Lecturer, University of Michigan
Ann Arbor, MI

Melissa C. Bergin, L.M.S., NBCT
Niskayuna High School
Niskayuna, NY

Rose Davenport, M.S.L.S., Ed.Specialist
Library Media Specialist
Pershing High School Library
Detroit, MI

Karen Imarisio, A.M.L.S.
Assistant Head of Adult Services
Bloomfield Twp. Public Library
Bloomfield Hills, MI

Nancy Larsen, M.L.S., M.S. Ed.
Library Media Specialist
Clarkston High School
Clarkston, MI

Marilyn Mast, M.I.L.S.
Kingswood Campus Librarian
Cranbrook Kingswood Upper School
Bloomfield Hills, MI

Rosemary Orlando, M.L.I.S.
Assistant Director
St. Clair Shores Public Library
St. Clair Shores, MI

Comments and Suggestions

We welcome your comments on *Defining Moments: Watergate* and suggestions for other events in U.S. history that warrant treatment in the *Defining Moments* series. Correspondence should be addressed to:

Editor, *Defining Moments*
Omnigraphics, Inc.
615 Griswold
Detroit, MI 48226
E-mail: editorial@omnigraphics.com

HOW TO USE THIS BOOK

Defining Moments: Watergate provides users with a detailed and authoritative overview of the Watergate scandal. The preparation and arrangement of this volume—and all other books in the *Defining Moments* series—reflect an emphasis on providing a thorough and objective account of events that shaped our nation, presented in an easy-to-use reference work.

Defining Moments: Watergate is divided into three primary sections. The first of these sections, the **Narrative Overview**, provides a detailed, factual account of Watergate's progression from a seemingly insignificant burglary into a scandal that brought down a presidency. It also explores the affair's lasting impact on America's political and cultural landscape.

The second section, **Biographies**, provides valuable biographical background on Watergate's leading figures, from President Richard M. Nixon himself to special prosecutor Archibald Cox and Watergate Committee chairman Sam Ervin. Each biography concludes with a list of sources for further information on the profiled individual.

The third section, **Primary Sources**, collects the most crucial documents of the Watergate era, including President Nixon's historic resignation speech, alongside documents that capture changing American perceptions of Watergate, such as *Time* Magazine's dramatic 1973 editorial, "Nixon Should Resign." Other primary sources featured in *Defining Moments: Watergate* include excerpts from official documents, papers and resolutions, speeches, letters, memoirs, editorials, and other important works.

Other valuable features in *Defining Moments: Watergate* include the following:

- Attribution and referencing of primary sources and other quoted material to help guide users to other valuable historical research resources.

- Glossary of Important People, Places, and Terms.

- Detailed Chronology of Watergate events with a *see reference* feature. Under this arrangement, events listed in the chronology include a reference to page numbers within the Narrative Overview wherein users can find additional information on the event in question.

- Photographs of the leading figures and major events of Watergate.

- Sources for Further Study, an annotated list of noteworthy Watergate-related works.

- Extensive bibliography of works consulted in the creation of this book, including books, periodicals, Internet sites, and videotape materials.

- A Subject Index.

IMPORTANT PEOPLE, PLACES, AND TERMS

Agnew, Spiro
Vice President of the United States from 1969 to 1973

Bernstein, Carl
Washington Post journalist who covered the Watergate scandal with colleague Bob Woodward

Butterfield, Alexander
White House aide who revealed the existence of Nixon's audiotaping system

Colson, Charles "Chuck"
Special Counsel to the President

Committee to Re-Elect the President (CRP or CREEP)
President Nixon's 1972 campaign organization

Cox, Archibald
First Watergate Special Prosecutor

CREEP
Unofficial acronym for Nixon's Committee to Re-Elect the President

CRP
Official acronym for Nixon's Committee to Re-Elect the President

Dash, Samuel
Chief Counsel for the Ervin Watergate Committee

Dean, John
White House Counsel in the Nixon Administration

Ehrlichman, John
Chief Domestic Policy Advisor to Nixon

Ervin, Sam
Senator who chaired the U.S. Senate investigation into Watergate

Executive Privilege
Doctrine that stipulates that the president has the right to keep military and diplomatic information secret from Congress and the public for national security reasons

Ford, Gerald R.
Vice President who became the 38th President of the U.S. after Nixon's resignation

Gray, L. Patrick
Acting Director of the FBI

Haig, Alexander
Nixon's second Chief of Staff

Haldeman, H. R.
Nixon's first Chief of Staff

Helms, Richard
Director of the Central Intelligence Agency (CIA)

Hunt, E. Howard
White House staffer and leader of the "plumbers unit"

Impeachment
Congressional process that provides for removal of the president from office if he is found guilty of "high crimes or misdemeanors"

Jaworski, Leon
Second Watergate Special Prosecutor

Liddy, G. Gordon
General counsel for the Committee to Re-Elect the President (CREEP) and leader of the "plumbers unit"

Magruder, Jeb
Deputy Director of the Committee to Re-Elect the President (CREEP)

McCord, James W., Jr.
Ex-CIA employee who participated in Watergate break-in

Mitchell, John N.
Attorney General who resigned to direct Nixon's re-election campaign

Nixon, Richard M.
37th President of the United States

Richardson, Elliot
Nixon Attorney General who resigned during the "Saturday Night Massacre"

Saturday Night Massacre
Media term for the evening of October 20, 1973, when White House actions triggered the departures of Attorney General Elliot Richardson, Assistant Attorney General William Ruckelshaus, and Special Prosecutor Archibald Cox

Sirica, John
Presiding federal court judge on the Watergate case

Subpoena
Judicial order that compels the recipient to testify in legal proceedings

Watergate
Hotel and office complex in Washington, D.C.; the site of a burglary by individuals with ties to President Nixon; a term that became synonymous with the national scandal and constitutional crisis that led to the resignation of President Nixon

Woodward, Bob
Washington Post journalist who covered the Watergate scandal with colleague Carl Bernstein

Ziegler, Ron
Press secretary during the Nixon administration

CHRONOLOGY

1968
November 5, 1968 – Richard Nixon wins the presidency with 43.4 percent of the popular vote. *See p. 4.*

1969
January 20, 1969 – Nixon inaugurated as 37th president of the United States. *See p. 4.*

1970
July 14, 1970 – Nixon approves the Huston plan, which expands domestic intelligence-gathering activities. *See p. 6.*

July 28, 1970 – Nixon rescinds approval of Huston plan because of opposition from FBI Director J. Edgar Hoover and Attorney General John Mitchell. *See p. 6.*

1971
June 13, 1971 – The *New York Times* begins publishing the Pentagon Papers, a secret history of the Vietnam War delivered to the *Times* by Daniel Ellsberg. *See p. 8.*

September 3-4, 1971 – White House "plumbers unit" led by aides G. Gordon Liddy and E. Howard Hunt, Jr., supervise burglary of office of Daniel Ellsberg's psychiatrist. *See p. 8.*

1972
March 1, 1972 – John Mitchell leaves Attorney General post to become director of the Committee to Re-Elect the President (CREEP).

April 27, 1972 – Former frontrunner Edmund S. Muskie withdraws from campaign for presidential nomination of Democratic Party. *See p. 12.*

June 17, 1972 – Five burglars arrested for break-in of Democratic National Committee headquarters at Watergate office and apartment complex in Washington, D.C. *See p. 16.*

June 20, 1972 – Nixon discusses the arrests of the burglars with campaign manager Mitchell and chief of staff H.R. Haldeman; record of the latter conversation is erased by famous 18 1/2 minute gap on Watergate tapes. *See p. 20.*

June 21, 1972 – Mitchell publicly declares that neither CREEP nor the White House are connected to the break-in in any way.

June 23, 1972 – Nixon and Haldeman agree to use the CIA to interfere with the FBI investigation into the Watergate break-in. The tape of this conversation comes to be seen by Watergate investigators as the "smoking gun" that proved Nixon lied about his early involvement in cover-up activities. *See p. 21.*

September 15, 1972 – Hunt, Liddy, and five Watergate burglars indicted on federal charges in Watergate case.

November 7, 1972 – Nixon and Vice-President Spiro Agnew win re-election with nearly 61 percent of popular vote and 97 percent of the electoral vote. *See p. 25.*

1973

January 8-30, 1973 – All seven men indicted for the Watergate burglary plead guilty or are convicted. *See p. 27.*

February 7, 1973 – The U.S. Senate votes 77-0 to establish a committee to investigate Watergate. *See p. 28.*

March 21, 1973 – A pivotal meeting takes place between Nixon and White House Counsel John Dean, a chief architect of Watergate cover-up. This conversation reveals Nixon's deep complicity in the cover-up. *See p. 29.*

March 23, 1973 – Judge John Sirica makes public a letter from one of the Watergate burglars charging that high-ranking officials were involved in an extensive Watergate cover-up. *See p. 29.*

April 30, 1973 – Nixon announces the resignations of Haldeman, John Ehrlichman, and Attorney General Richard Kleindeinst, and the firing of Dean. *See p. 33.*

May 4, 1973 – Nixon announces the appointment of Alexander Haig as interim chief of staff. *See p. 34.*

May 17, 1973 – The Senate Watergate Committee chaired by North Carolina Democat Sam Irvin begins its nationally televised hearings. *See p. 36.*

May 18, 1973 – Archibald Cox is named Special Prosecutor by new Attorney General Elliot Richardson. *See p. 35.*

May 22, 1973 – Nixon issues public statement in which he explicitly denies any knowledge of the Watergate burglary or cover-up. *See p. 36.*

May 25, 1973 – Richardson and Cox both take their formal oaths for their respective offices.

June 25-29, 1973 – Dean testifies before the Senate Watergate Committee that Nixon was an active participant in the Watergate cover-up. *See p. 38.*

July 13, 1973 – White House aide Alexander Butterfield reveals the existence of Nixon's taping system in an interview with investigators. *See p. 43.*

July 16, 1973 – Butterfield confirms the existence of the taping system in public testimony, triggering a protracted struggle for possession of the tapes. *See p. 44.*

July 23, 1973 – Cox subpoenas the recordings of nine White House tapes. *See p. 46.*

July 25, 1973 – Nixon refuses to turn over the nine subpoenaed tapes, citing executive privilege. *See p. 46.*

August 29, 1973 – Sirica rules that the White House must turn over the subpoenaed tapes; the Nixon administration announces its intention to appeal the ruling. *See p. 46.*

September 29, 1973 – Nixon secretary Rose Mary Woods begins transcribing some of the White House tapes.

October 10, 1973 – Vice President Agnew resigns in disgrace. *See p. 51.*

October 20, 1973 – At Nixon's insistence, Special Prosecutor Archibald Cox is fired; Attorney General Elliot Richardson and Deputy Attorney General William Ruckelshaus both resign over Cox's dismissal; departure of the three men is described as "Saturday Night Massacre" by stunned news media. *See p. 48.*

October 23-24, 1973 – Nearly two dozen bills are introduced in Congress calling for an impeachment investigation in conjunction with Watergate. *See p. 50.*

November 1, 1973 – Leon Jaworski officially succeeds Archibald Cox as Special Prosecutor in the Watergate affair. *See p. 51.*

November 4, 1973 – Republican Senator Edward W. Brooke of Massachusetts calls on the president to resign.

November 21, 1973 – White House lawyers disclose to Judge Sirica that one of the subpoenaed tapes has an 18 1/2 minute gap on it; Sirica makes this news public later the same day. *See p. 51.*

December 6, 1973 – Gerald Ford sworn in as the 40th Vice President of the United States. *See p. 52.*

December 8, 1973 – Judge Sirica listens to the first seven subpoenaed Watergate tapes. *See p. 52.*

December 12, 1973 – Special Prosecutor Jaworski receives portions of the seven subpoenaed tapes. *See p. 52.*

1974

January 4, 1974 – James St. Clair appointed as chief Nixon counsel for the Watergate defense.

January 15, 1974 – Technical experts report that 18 1/2 minute gap on the June 20 Watergate tape was created by five separate manual erasures.

February 6, 1974 – House of Representatives votes to begin formal impeachment inquiry by a 410-4 vote. *See p. 53.*

March 1, 1974 – Grand jury indicts seven officials in the Watergate cover-up, including Haldeman, Ehrlichman, and Colson. Nixon is named an unindicted co-conspirator by the grand jury. *See p. 54.*

April 11, 1974 – The House Judiciary Committee subpoenas 42 White House tapes.

April 18, 1974 – Special Prosecutor Jaworski subpoenas 64 White House tapes.

April 29, 1974 – Nixon announces his decision to provide edited transcripts of the subpoenaed tapes, but holds firm to his refusal to release the tapes themselves. Transcripts are released the following day. *See p. 54.*

May 9, 1974 – House Minority Leader John J. Rhodes states that Nixon should think about resigning.

May 24, 1974 – Jaworski appeals directly to the Supreme Court for a ruling on his subpoena for 64 White House tapes.

July 24, 1974 – The Supreme Court issues a unanimous ruling that Nixon must turn over the 64 tapes subpoenaed by Jaworski. *See p. 56.*

July 27, 1974 – The House Judiciary Committee passes the first article of impeachment by a 27-11 vote. *See p. 57.*

July 29, 1974 – The House Judiciary Committee passes the second article of impeachment by 22-10 vote. *See p. 58.*

July 30, 1974 – The House Judiciary Committee passes the third article of impeachment by 21-17 vote. *See p. 58.*

August 5, 1974 – The White House releases transcripts of tapes, including the infamous "Smoking Gun" tape of June 23, 1972. *See p. 58.*

August 6, 1974 – All Republican members of House Judiciary Committee announce their intention to vote to impeach Nixon. *See p. 61.*

August 8, 1974 – Nixon announces decision to resign in nationally televised address. *See p. 63.*

August 9, 1974 – Nixon resigns and Gerald R. Ford is sworn in as president in Oval Office ceremony. *See p. 68.*

September 8, 1974 – Ford grants a full pardon to Nixon. *See p. 69.*

1994

April 22, 1994 – Nixon dies in New York City. *See p. 77.*

PROLOGUE

As the sun rose over the United States on the morning of August 8, 1974, Americans woke up to the knowledge that a protracted battle waged at the highest levels of government was about to draw to a close. For the previous two years, President Richard Milhous Nixon and his aides had engaged in increasingly desperate political combat and legal maneuvering to save themselves from a scandal known as Watergate. But after months of dramatic revelations about criminal activity in the Nixon White House, the president had finally admitted defeat. He had announced his intention to resign the presidency in a nationally televised speech later that evening.

The news that Nixon was planning to resign aroused emotions of anger, sorrow, and disbelief across the country, but these feelings were particularly powerful in the nation's capital, Washington, D.C. Much of the Watergate struggle had taken place in the corridors of the White House and Congress. In addition, the Washington press corps had played a major role in uncovering and publicizing the illegal activities that brought down Nixon and his inner circle of aides.

Elizabeth Drew was one of the many journalists who spent months of their careers covering the unfolding Watergate scandal. In the following excerpt from her book *Washington Journal: The Events of 1973-1974*, Drew recalls how she felt during those final hours in Washington, D.C., just before the first presidential resignation in U.S. history:

> There is already some talk about "what the historians will say"—the historians, those unknown people who in the future will have the franchise to interpret what is going on now. We tend to assume that out of their years of accumulation of fact they will sift the truth—a truer truth than any we can hope to grasp. They will have many more facts, and they will have what

is called "perspective" (which means they will not be trapped in the biases of our day and can freely write in the biases of *their* day—can find what they are looking for). But I wonder if they will really understand what it was like. Will they know how it felt to go through what we have gone through? Will they know how it felt to be stunned—again and again—as we learned what had been done by people in power? Will they know how it felt to be shocked, ashamed, amused by the revelations—will they understand the difficulty of sorting out the madcap from the macabre? ...Can they conceivably understand how it felt as we watched, on our television screen, our President say, "I am not a crook"? ...Will they understand how it felt—as it did last fall at the time the President fired Special Prosecutor Cox, and on several later occasions—when it seemed that there were no checks on power? Will they understand how degrading it was to watch a President being run to ground? Will they know how it was to feel in the thrall of this strange man, who seemed to answer only to himself? Knowing the conclusion, as they will, will they understand how difficult, frightening, and fumbling the struggle really was?

Chapter 1
EVENTS LEADING UP TO THE WATERGATE SCANDAL

⟿⟦∫⟧⟾

Watergate did not begin when CREEP operatives broke into Democratic headquarters in 1972. It began when Nixon took office, armed with his private slush fund, prepared to do battle by fair means and foul against his enemies.

– Historian Melvin Small

The political scandal known as Watergate flared to life on June 17, 1972. That evening, a group of people linked to Republican President Richard Nixon's re-election organization committed a burglary. The burglars were caught inside the offices of the Democratic Party's national headquarters, located in the Watergate hotel complex in Washington, D.C. After the arrests, Nixon and his top aides initiated a massive cover-up of White House links to the burglars. This cover-up was eventually exposed by separate investigations carried out by Congressional investigators, special prosecutors, and journalists.

The revelations about the nature and extent of Nixon's involvement in the Watergate scandal stunned and angered the American public. Support for Nixon evaporated, both in Washington, D.C. and in the court of public opinion. Recognizing that his presidency was doomed, Nixon became the first president in U.S. history to resign from office.

Nixon's Controversial Political Career

Some historians have commented that the Watergate scandal was a strangely fitting climax to Nixon's long political career (see Nixon biography, p. 112). In fact, many observed that his life in politics had been shrouded in controversy from the very beginning. In 1946 he won a seat in the California delegation of the U.S. House of Representatives—his first run for public office—by waging a brutally negative campaign against his Democratic opponent, repeatedly slandering him as a Communist sympathizer. In 1950 he used the same sort of ruthless campaign tactics to win a seat in the U.S. Senate. And from 1953 to 1961, when he served as vice president in the administration of President Dwight D. Eisenhower, Nixon polished his reputation as a skilled, battle-hardened politician.

Nixon's combative ways and conservative political beliefs won him many admirers—and an equal number of detractors. In November 1960, he ran as the Republican nominee for president, but narrowly lost to Democratic candidate John F. Kennedy. By that point, Nixon "was the most hated and feared man in America—and next to Eisenhower himself, the most admired and wanted," stated historian Stephen Ambrose in *Nixon: Ruin and Recovery, 1973-1990.*

When Nixon ran for governor of California in 1962 and lost, many observers thought that his political career was over. But he staged a dramatic comeback to earn the Republican Party's presidential nomination in 1968. Later that year he defeated Democratic candidate Hubert Humphrey and independent candidate George Wallace to claim the White House.

Nixon's Abuses of Power

Nixon became president at a critical moment in American history. When he took the oath of office in January 1969, the United States was profoundly divided. American neighborhoods, workplaces, newsrooms, and schools were wracked by deeply felt differences on the Vietnam War, civil rights, societal values, and other issues. These clashes bred so much anger and resentment among different races, social classes, and generational groups that the basic fabric of American life sometimes seemed under threat. Indeed, Nixon was inaugurated in an atmosphere of significant cynicism and suspicion toward civil and social institutions. He also assumed office during a period of intense partisanship between the nation's two chief political parties, which were on opposite sides of many of the issues confronting the nation.

Many historians believe that the poisonous, bitter political environment that existed when Nixon became president brought out the worst aspects of his personality. Nixon was an intelligent and hardworking man with vast experience in the rough-and-tumble world of American politics. But he also pos-

Nixon made a triumphant return to national politics with his 1968 presidential election victory.

sessed a distrustful, insecure, and vindictive nature, and these aspects of his personality led him to take actions that ultimately destroyed his presidency.

As Nixon settled into the Oval Office, he responded to the nation's turmoil by embracing the same sort of ruthless political tactics that had served him so well over the years. Determined to keep the upper hand over his political enemies, Nixon and his aides routinely engaged in a wide range of illegal activities prior to the Watergate affair. "Some of these activities [Nixon] inherited; others he initiated," wrote historian Keith W. Olson in *Watergate*. "Nixon accepted these illegal activities as an inherent power, risk free since secrecy would prevent discovery."

At first, leaders in the antiwar movement were the main focus of this activity. As time passed, however, the Nixon administration also identified certain journalists, organized labor leaders, Democratic legislators, and private citizens as threats. Many of the criminal actions launched against these individuals were undertaken for the same purpose as the Watergate break-in: to compromise, destroy, or otherwise gain political advantage over perceived enemies. And it was this history of criminal activity—which Nixon Attorney General John Mitchell later dubbed the "White House horrors"—that Nixon and his aides were most determined to conceal when the Watergate burglary occurred.

The Watergate investigation eventually revealed a wide array of criminal activities sanctioned by the Nixon White House. These activities included secret surveillance of political opponents; illegal wiretapping of reporters and administration members; manufacturing of false documents to support Nixon administration policy goals; burglaries and other illegal activities designed to uncover information that could be used to smear the reputations of opponents; and use of the Internal Revenue Service (IRS) and other governmental agencies to threaten and punish Americans on Nixon's "enemies list."

Nixon's "Enemies List"

In 1970 White House aide Tom Huston led the development of an intelligence-gathering scheme that became known as "the Huston Plan." This plan proposed to reorganize the nation's principal intelligence-gathering agencies—most notably the Federal Bureau of Investigation (FBI) and the Central Intelligence Agency (CIA)—so that damaging information on White House foes would be funneled directly to Nixon and his closest aides. Nixon was receptive to the idea, stating "we must develop a plan which will enable us to curtail the illegal activities of those who are determined to destroy our society."

FBI Director J. Edgar Hoover ultimately managed to kill the Huston Plan, but the White House's desire to use its power to smite political enemies remained strong. In August 1971 White House Counsel John Dean proposed to create a formal "enemies list" (see Dean biography, p. 92). "This memorandum addresses the matter of how we can maximize the fact of our incumbency in dealing with persons known to be active in their opposition to our administration," wrote Dean. "Stated a bit more bluntly—how we can use the available federal machinery to screw our political enemies."

Dean's memo proceeded to lay out a framework for maintaining the list. "Key members of the staff should be requested to inform us as to who they feel we should be giving a hard time.... The project coordinator should then determine what sorts of dealings these individuals have with the federal government and how we can best screw them (e.g., grant availability, federal contracts, litigation, prosecution, etc.)."

Charles Colson: The Nixon Administration's Controversial "Evil Genius"

Charles W. Colson carried out numerous illegal activities on behalf of the Nixon White House.

As special counsel to the president from 1969 to 1973, Charles "Chuck" Colson became known within the Nixon administration as the resident "evil genius," a reference to his talent for developing unethical but effective schemes against White House enemies.

Born in Boston on October 16, 1931, he served in the Marines, studied law, and became a partner in two high-powered law firms before entering politics. After joining the White House at the beginning of Nixon's first term, he became notorious for his loyalty to the president and his willingness to do virtually anything to advance the administration's agenda.

In 1974 Colson served seven months in prison in Alabama after pleading guilty to obstruction of justice in the Daniel Ellsberg case. Colson reportedly underwent a dramatic religious conversion before and during his imprisonment. Upon his release, he published an autobiography, *Born Again* (1976), describing his conversion experience. That same year, he founded Prison Fellowship Ministries, a volunteer-based organization that brings Christian teachings to inmates and their families.

In the three decades since Watergate occurred, Colson has remained deeply involved in Christian ministry and criminal justice reforms. His Prison Fellowship Ministries remains one of the largest evangelical outreach organizations of its kind, and in 1993 Colson won the prestigious Templeton Prize for Progress in Religion. Colson has also written numerous books of fiction and nonfiction.

Charles Colson, who formally served as special counsel to the president, took over development of the list (see "Charles Colson: The Nixon Administration's Controversial 'Evil Genius,'" p. 7). Within a few months, the number of identified "enemies" had grown to over 200 people. People on the list included actor Paul Newman, broadcaster Daniel Schorr, Democratic lawmakers Ted Kennedy and Walter Mondale, and the presidents of several of the nation's leading universities and foundations.

Dean and other Nixon aides later described the list as a mere "exercise" that never resulted in any hostile actions against the people on it. But a number of people on the list were subjected to repeated tax audits from the Internal Revenue Service and other forms of harassment as a direct result of White House machinations.

The existence of the enemies list was not revealed until mid-1973, during Dean's testimony before the Senate committee investigating the Watergate affair. Years after his resignation, Nixon insisted that the importance of the list had been greatly exaggerated. But some people who learned that their names had been on the list found it to be a scary revelation. Stanley Kutler noted in the *Wars of Watergate* that one person on the list, *Washington Post* attorney Edward Bennett Williams, was audited for three consecutive years. When he learned that he had been targeted by the White House, Williams initially regarded it as a "badge of honor." But he also admitted that it was frightening to think that the "President of the United States [was] obsessed with the idea of wreaking some kind of revenge against me."

The most infamous of the pre-Watergate illegal activities took place on the night of September 3-4, 1971. At that time a secret White House political outfit known as the "plumbers unit" burglarized the offices of psychiatrist Lewis Fielding. Fielding's office was targeted because his clients included Daniel Ellsberg, a Pentagon official responsible for the public release of the so-called Pentagon Papers. The Pentagon Papers was a secret history of the Vietnam War that had been published by the *New York Times* in the summer of 1971 over the strong objections of the Nixon White House. This account revealed that four successive administrations had deceived the American public about various aspects of the conflict.

The weekend ransacking of Fielding's offices was carried out by the same men who later participated in the Watergate break-in. The Fielding burglary was a failure on multiple levels. First, it failed to find information that could be used to humiliate or discredit Ellsberg. And second, the Nixon administration's involvement in the Fielding break-in became a leading rationale for launching the Watergate cover-up. The White House feared that if investigators learned the full story of the Watergate burglary, they would also discover its role in the Fielding burglary.

Nixon's First Term

Nixon's political struggles during his first term in office, from 1969 to 1972, also laid the groundwork for the Watergate crisis. Nixon's predecessor in the White House, Democrat Lyndon B. Johnson, had been so badly battered by the turmoil of the 1960s—especially the seemingly endless Vietnam War—that he had declined to seek re-election. When he left office, the presidency had been deeply scarred and weakened by the seemingly intractable problems dividing American society.

As president, Nixon repeatedly clashed with the Democrat-controlled Congress. The two sides differed on a wide range of issues, from social and fiscal policy to strategies for ending American involvement in Vietnam. The results of the 1970 Congressional elections, in which the Democratic Party increased its majorities in both the Senate and the House of Representatives, marked a further setback in Nixon's attempt to stamp his imprint on American policies and institutions.

Still, Nixon's first four years earned him a passing grade from the majority of the American public, in large measure because the White House consciously projected an image of him as a strong and resolute leader. "For much of Nixon's first term, he and his aides labored to portray him as the President he believed himself, or desired, to be," wrote historian Stanley Kutler in *Wars of Watergate*. "And to a great extent, that was the President that the media reported and projected. Richard Nixon had his detractors and perennial critics, but neither they nor the American public had any sense or proof of a darker side to him or to the acts of his Administration."

Gearing Up for the 1972 Election

By 1971, the Nixon administration was already looking ahead to the following year's presidential election. "Nixon had a hard time with Congress his first term; a lot of things he proposed didn't go through," recalled former

Nixon secretary of commerce Maurice Stans in an interview with Gerald and Deborah Strober for *Nixon: An Oral History of His Presidency*. "His basic concept was that he had to win big to increase the size of his mandate from the people. That idea permeated his campaign organization; it permeated the White House; and I think everybody was working on the idea that the bigger the vote, the better the next four years were going to be."

Nixon was eager to use a big election victory as a tool to advance his domestic and foreign policy agenda. Top priorities in his agenda included improving relations with China—which he had visited on a historic diplomatic trip in 1971—and the Soviet Union. He also wanted to withdraw the United States from Vietnam "with peace and honor," reshuffle domestic spending priorities, and ensure a return to "law and order" on the home front. But he also focused on the election for more personal reasons. By earning a second term, Nixon would be able to savor a major victory over the many politicians, civic leaders, and journalists whom he perceived as enemies.

Chapter 2

THE BREAK-IN

—⟪⟫—

There was trouble. Some people got caught. I'll probably be going to jail.

– G. Gordon Liddy to his wife, upon returning home after the botched Watergate burglary

During President Nixon's first term, his administration showed a clear willingness to engage in illegal activities that could provide political benefits to the White House. This attitude extended to the campaign to re-elect Nixon as well. By the end of his first term, many members of his administration were also working on his reelection campaign. As the November 1972 presidential election drew closer, Nixon and his closest aides—including H. R. Haldeman (Chief of Staff), John Ehrlichman (Director of White House Domestic Policy), and John Mitchell (Attorney General who became the head of Nixon's 1972 re-election campaign)—approved major intelligence-gathering activities focused on disrupting or embarrassing the campaigns of his potential presidential rivals (see biographies on Haldeman, p. 102; Ehrlichman, p. 96; and Mitchell, p. 108).

Many of these schemes involved criminal conduct, but Nixon rationalized the activities as legitimate political strategy. He also viewed these efforts as justified payback for years of punishment at the hands of Democratic political opponents. "[I] insisted to Haldeman and others …that in this campaign we were finally in a position to have someone doing to the opposition what they had done to us," Nixon wrote in *RN: The Memoirs of Richard Nixon*. "They knew that this time I wanted the leading Democrats annoyed, harassed and embarrassed—as I had been in the past…. I told my staff that we should come up with the kind of imaginative dirty tricks that our Democratic opponents used against us and others so effectively in previous campaigns."

Not surprisingly, Nixon's inner circle of aides and advisors followed these instructions with enthusiasm. Eager to please the president, they adopted the same hostile attitude toward political opponents as their boss, devising ruthless political strategies that would advance Nixon's goals. As Watergate figure Jeb Magruder later wrote in *An American Life*, "the climate of fear and suspicion" that descended over the White House during Nixon's years in office "started with the President himself" and filtered down throughout his administration.

Some of the "dirty tricks" conjured up by the White House and the Committee to Re-Elect the President (officially abbreviated as CRP but most often referred to as CREEP) amounted to little more than the sort of pranks that high school kids pull on one another. For example, operatives were fond of ordering large numbers of unwanted pizzas to Democratic political rallies. They also used stink bombs to disrupt picnics held on behalf of Democratic candidates. Agents even made middle-of-the-night telephone calls to prospective Democratic voters, falsely claiming to be supporters of one of the Democratic candidates. But other maneuvers were much uglier in nature. Republican operatives—most notably Donald Segretti—forged letters in the names of various Democratic leaders, recruited spies within the various campaigns, distributed flyers advertising nonexistent rallies and other events for candidates, and manufactured vicious rumors about the personal histories and sexual preferences of leading candidates (see "Liddy's Gemstone Program," p. 14).

All of the leading Democratic candidates were on the receiving end of this treatment, which was carried out by three distinct operations at one point. But the biggest victim may have been Senator Ed Muskie of Maine. Muskie was widely seen as the front-runner for the Democratic presidential nomination, but he faltered badly and dropped out of the race in April 1972.

The failure of Muskie's candidacy delighted Nixon aides, but the role of the dirty tricks campaign in his failed bid for the Democratic nomination has since been sharply disputed. Some historians believe that it may have been a significant factor. Others contend that the tactics had the "weight of a feather," as historian Theodore White wrote in *The Making of the President 1972*, in their impact on the race for the nomination.

Republican "dirty tricks" helped derail the presidential candidacy of Democratic Senator Edmund S. Muskie in 1972.

Break-In at the Watergate

In May 1972 the drive to gain advantage over political opponents by fair means or foul took a fateful turn. G. Gordon Liddy, who was CREEP's general counsel—and its director of intelligence gathering—devised a plan to bug and burglarize the offices of Lawrence O'Brien. O'Brien was the chairman of the Democratic National Committee (DNC), the party's national coordinating and fundraising body for the upcoming elections. On the night of May 26, Liddy and his colleague E. Howard Hunt (a former CIA agent who worked on several secret White House projects) sent a team of Cuban refugees headed by a man named Bernard Barker to break into the Watergate hotel and office complex in Washington, D.C., home of the DNC's national headquarters. This first attempt failed.

13

Liddy's Gemstone Program

G. Gordon Liddy, a former FBI agent turned lawyer, began working as general counsel and director of intelligence gathering for the Committee to Re-Elect the President (CREEP) on December 13, 1971. Within a few weeks of taking the post, he had developed an ambitious security and intelligence plan called Gemstone for the White House's consideration.

On January 27, 1972, Liddy presented the Gemstone plan to Attorney General John Mitchell. The Attorney General is the head of the Department of Justice and is the chief law enforcement officer of the U.S. government. (This was shortly before Mitchell resigned his government law enforcement post in March 1972 to assume the reins of CREEP.) White House counsel John Dean and CREEP Deputy Director Jeb Magruder also attended the January 1972 meeting. Liddy's proposed program, which came with an estimated price tag of $1 million, included burglaries, wiretapping, sabotage, kidnapping, and the use of prostitutes for political blackmail.

At the conclusion of Liddy's presentation, Mitchell commented wryly that Gemstone was not quite what he had in mind. A week or so later, Liddy returned with a revised plan that concentrated on break-ins, wire-

tapping, and other types of electronic surveillance of opponents. After further discussion, Mitchell approved a modest ($250,000 budget) version of Liddy's scheme. Months later, Mitchell voiced profound regret for this decision, saying that he should have thrown Liddy and his plan out the window. After receiving the green light to proceed, Liddy and White House aides agreed to make Lawrence O'Brien, head of the Democratic National Committee, the first target of the illegal campaign. The subsequent attempt to bug O'Brien's offices at the Watergate Hotel is what set the Watergate scandal in motion.

G. Gordon Liddy, one of the masterminds of the Watergate break-in.

The Watergate Hotel Complex, headquarters of the Democratic National Committee during the 1972 elections.

The burglars made a second unsuccessful bid to sneak into the DNC offices on May 27. One night later, Barker and his associates—Virgilio Gonzalez, Eugenio Martinez, and Frank Sturgis, along with a CREEP employee named James McCord—finally gained entrance into the DNC offices on their third attempt. They photographed a variety of DNC documents and planted wiretaps on the telephones of O'Brien and DNC staffer R. Spencer Oliver. Initially, Liddy and his men believed that the mission had been successful. Over the next several days, however, they realized that one of the wiretaps was not working correctly.

In the early morning of June 17, 1972, Barker, McCord, and the other members of the burglary team carried out yet another break-in of DNC headquarters in order to fix the malfunctioning wiretap. Liddy and Hunt monitored their movements from another part of the Watergate complex. It was during this nighttime foray that a hotel security guard named Frank Wills detected signs of intruders. He promptly called the police, who arrested the burglars.

When police arrested Barker, McCord, and the others, they confiscated a wide range of expensive gadgets, including cameras and electronic surveillance equipment. They also discovered that the burglars were carrying a large number of $100 bills. This money would later be traced to CREEP, Nixon's re-election committee. As the burglars were booked at the local jail, Hunt and Liddy set about destroying evidence of CREEP's links to the crime. They also secretly used CREEP funds to provide lawyers for the arrested men. But by this time, the veil of secrecy that had covered the Nixon administration's many illegal activities was already beginning to unravel. Mere hours after the burglars' arrests, FBI investigators and journalists were tracking down leads that eventually linked both the White House and CREEP to the break-in.

Years later, historians still debate who gave the actual order to break into the Watergate complex. Living individuals associated with the scandal argue about it as well. Liddy, for instance, has long claimed that White House Counsel John Dean was actually the driving force behind the Watergate burglary, a charge that Dean has repeatedly denied. Many others believe that the culprit was John Mitchell, who managed Nixon's 1972 re-election campaign. This was the conclusion drawn by Carl Bernstein and Bob Woodward, the *Washington Post* reporters whose investigation of the break-in and subsequent cover-up brought several important aspects of the Watergate affair to public light. Other individuals cited as the moving force behind the break-in range from Nixon himself to CREEP deputy director Jeb Magruder to someone from the CIA.

"This is the startling thing about Watergate," stated Nixon press secretary Ron Ziegler in a 1994 interview with Gerald and Deborah Hart Strober for *Nixon: An Oral History of His Presidency*. "It's 20 years later, and I still don't know who ordered the break-in; certainly no one has admitted that they ordered it. Did the president? Did Dean? Did Magruder? It is an extraordinary set of circumstances; why doesn't somebody just come out and say, 'I ordered it,' so we can clear all of this up." Thus far, however, compelling evidence about the identity of the person who ordered the break-in has yet to be found. In addition, no evidence has yet been found that Nixon had any prior knowledge that the Watergate break-in was going to occur. It was his actions *after* the break-in that ultimately led to his resignation.

Muted Initial Reaction to the Break-In

In the first few days following the arrest of the Watergate burglars, there was little indication that the story would erupt into a major scandal. When White House press secretary Ron Ziegler described it as a "third-rate burglary," his words reflected the views of most observers. Even journalist Bob Woodward has acknowledged that he first viewed the break-in as a minor story. But when the press discovered that Watergate burglar James McCord was a former CIA employee on the payroll of Nixon's campaign organization, a few newspapers—most notably the *Washington Post*—doggedly pursued the story. "It's like getting in a bath and turning the water hotter and hotter; you don't feel the incremental increase in temperature, because it's going up so slowly and you're already so hot," Woodward told the Strobers. "I mean hot, in the sense that the story immediately had CIA people, rubber gloves, hundred dollar bills. So at eleven or twelve o'clock that morning [of June 18] in the office, I had a very different impression of the story than I did when I was awakened. If you were to graph it, it just kept going up and up and up." For the next several months, the *Washington Post* pursued its investigation of the burglary and subsequent cover-up even as most other news media remained on the sidelines.

In the White House, meanwhile, initial reaction to the arrest of the White House burglars also was mild. Haldeman later admitted that he and other staff members did not recognize the gravity of the situation. The break in, he recalled, was "really only one of maybe 15 things we were honing in on that day." Nixon later stated that he learned of the break-in on June 18, when he read about it in the newspaper while in Key Biscayne, Florida. Over the next few days, aides informed him that a member of his CREEP re-election campaign organization—McCord—had been among those arrested, and that other links existed between the burglary team and the White House.

Armed with this information, Nixon decided to launch a cover-up of White House and CREEP links to the burglary. "My motive was pure political containment," he declared in a televised interview with David Frost in 1978. "And political containment is not a corrupt motive." In his memoirs, Nixon explained his decision to take part in a cover-up in more detail. "My reaction to the Watergate break-in was completely pragmatic," he wrote in *RN*. "If it was also cynical, it was a cynicism born of experience. I had been in politics too long, and seen everything from dirty tricks to vote fraud. I could not muster much moral outrage over a political bugging."

Chapter 3
THE COVER-UP

—◦◦◦◦◦◦◦—

I don't believe the White House can stand a wide-open investigation.... There are all kinds of things over there that could blow up in our face.

— White House Counsel John Dean

After the Watergate burglars were arrested, people involved in the break-in hoped that the botched burglary would be seen as a minor event of no great importance. But the FBI investigation into the Watergate break-in quickly emerged as a matter of serious concern to officials in the White House and Nixon's re-election campaign. The Democratic National Committee (DNC) publicly accused the Committee to Re-Elect the President (CRP or CREEP) of involvement in the Watergate burglary. The DNC also filed a $1 million civil lawsuit against CREEP.

In the meantime, the *Washington* Post reported within two days of the break-in that the FBI had found suspicious links between the burglars and the Nixon White House. Specifically, the newspaper reported links between the burglars and White House consultant E. Howard Hunt, who had co-organized the burglary team with G. Gordon Liddy. White House aides reluctantly concluded that it was only a matter of time until the FBI discovered that all the burglars had been paid with CREEP funds.

These developments prompted high-level White House and CREEP officials to huddle for a series of tense meetings and telephone conversations. During the course of these meetings, participants expressed deep concerns that the FBI investigation into the Watergate affair might expose other illegal activities involving the White House. They also discussed the potential political damage if those criminal activities were revealed to the general public. Given the high stakes involved, a decision was made to launch a massive cover-up.

Years later, participants in the scandal recalled that a cover-up seemed like the only viable option they had. "At some point …I realized that this was not just hard-nosed politics, this was a crime that could destroy us all," recalled Jeb Magruder in *An American Life,* his memoir of the Watergate scandal. "The cover-up, thus, was immediate and automatic; no one ever considered that there could *not* be a cover-up. It seemed inconceivable that with our political power we could not erase this mistake we had made."

The Cover-Up Begins

White House and CREEP officials immediately took several steps to cover up their links to the Watergate break-in. They destroyed documents and other potentially incriminating materials. In addition, they arranged bribes to ensure the silence of the men arrested in connection with Watergate. In fact, secret "hush money" payments were made to all the Watergate defendants through the remainder of 1972 and into early 1973.

Meanwhile, White House aides John Dean, H. R. Haldeman, and John Ehrlichman schemed with Nixon to stop the FBI investigation into the Watergate break-in. Within a week of the break-in, Nixon met with Chief of Staff Haldeman on multiple occasions to discuss the worrisome Watergate issue. Unbeknownst to Haldeman, these conversations were recorded on a secret taping system installed by Nixon in the Oval Office. When the existence of these tapes became publically known in July 1973, the Nixon White House waged a protracted but futile effort to keep them out of the hands of Watergate investigators. The release of the tapes doomed Nixon, for they revealed his deep complicity in the cover up.

On June 20—three days after the break-in—Nixon spoke with Haldeman about supressing the FBI investigation and raising money for the burglars. The tapes of this meeting also included a mysterious $18\frac{1}{2}$ minute gap in the recording. This portion of the tape is widely believed to have contained material that would have been extremely damaging to the president (Haleman later claimed that Nixon made the erasure himself).

During a June 23 meeting, Haldeman warned Nixon that "the FBI is not under control." Determined to derail the FBI investigation, Nixon and Halde-

President Nixon (right) and aides H. R. Haldeman (seated left) and John Ehrlichman (seated center) conspired to hide White House involvement in the Watergate burglary. Staffer Dwight Chapin (standing) was a minor figure in the cover-up.

man agreed to recruit the CIA to put the brakes on the FBI inquiry. Nixon and Haldeman persuaded CIA Director Richard Helms and other agency officials to pressure Acting FBI Director L. Patrick Gray to back off from the Watergate investigation. Months later, the release of the tape of this June 23 meeting made it clear that Nixon had taken a leading role in covering up White House and CREEP involvement in the Watergate affair. Today, the tape of the Nixon-Haldeman conversations of June 23, 1972, continues to be known as the "smoking gun" that proved Nixon's guilt (see "The 'Smoking Gun' Conversation Between Nixon and Haldeman," p. 132).

Acting FBI Director Gray, meanwhile, struggled with his response to the CIA warning. Unaware that Nixon himself wanted the FBI investigation reined in, he assumed that the warning originated with mid-level White House aides who were somehow involved in the break-in. At one point he even warned Nixon that members of his staff were trying to use the FBI and CIA in illegal ways that could "mortally wound" his presidency.

Ultimately, Gray never imposed dramatic new restrictions on the agency's investigation. He may have recognized that such a directive would outrage investigating agents and raise suspicions about his motives. But he compromised the investigation in other ways. For example, he routinely gave Dean access to classified FBI documents pertaining to the Watergate investigation. In addition, he destroyed potentially valuable evidence taken from burglar E. Howard Hunt's safe.

Watergate Issue Fails to Catch Fire with Voters

During the summer of 1972 the Nixon White House managed to keep its distance from the Watergate investigation. But this did not mean that Nixon and his aides lost interest in the subject. Instead, Nixon and his staff spent a good deal of time speculating about how they could avoid being stained by the investigation (see "John Dean Recalls the Early Days of the Watergate Cover-Up," p. 129). Often, their conversations reflected the stress of maintaining the cover-up. At one point, for example, Nixon declared that if bribery failed to buy the silence of the men implicated in the Watergate burglary, he would consider promising clemency. "I'll pardon the bastards," he blurted in a June 30 meeting. But as the weeks passed by without major incident, the president and his inner circle began to feel more confident. "[The investigation] has been kept away from the White House and of course completely from the President," Haldeman assured Nixon on September 15.

But the Watergate investigation did not completely vanish from public view. *Washington Post* reporters Carl Bernstein and Bob Woodward filed a series of stories on the subject during the summer and fall of 1972. As they produced these reports, the journalists confirmed the results of their exhaustive detective work with a mysterious informant they nicknamed "Deep Throat." This shadowy figure, who is believed to have been an official in the Nixon administration, did not volunteer new information on the Watergate break-in or cover-up. But he did confirm information the reporters discovered elsewhere, and his encouragement boosted their morale at several tense points in their investigation. More than three decades after Nixon's resignation, the identity of Deep Throat remains a closely guarded secret (see "Who Was Deep Throat?" p. 24).

Washington Post reporters Carl Bernstein (left) and Bob Woodward (right) zealously pursued the Watergate story from the outset.

The stories filed by Woodward and Bernstein in the *Washington Post* suggested possible White House involvement in the break-in and raised the possibility of a cover-up. But few other newspapers pursued the story with any real energy. From June 17 (the date of the final Watergate break-in) to November 7 (when the 1972 presidential election was held), Nixon held a total of four press conferences. During the course of these meetings with the press, journalists asked him a total of three questions about Watergate. "Reporters who covered the president obviously considered the subject of marginal importance," observed historian Keith W. Olson in *Watergate*. "Nixon's explicit language, his denial of prior knowledge, and his description of the intensity of the investigations seemed convincing."

Who Was Deep Throat?

One of the great mysteries of the Watergate scandal is the identity of "Deep Throat," the White House insider who helped *Washington Post* reporters Bob Woodward and Carl Bernstein pursue their investigation of the Watergate break-in and cover-up. Some historians and politicians from the Watergate era believe that Deep Throat—named after a famous pornographic movie of the early 1970s—was a composite of different sources. Others contend that he was a fictional character invented to increase public interest in *All the President's Men,* the best-selling book about Watergate published by Woodward and Bernstein in 1974. There are several other possibilities mentioned by historians, journalists, legislators, and various people associated with Watergate: Nixon speechwriters Pat Buchanan and Raymond Price, National Security Advisor Henry Kissinger, FBI officials Patrick Gray and Mark Felt, Nixon campaigner John Sears, and presidential advisor David Gergen.

People investigating the identity of Deep Throat note that he only confirmed or denied allegations the reporters had already learned—he never provided new information of which the journalists were unaware. By limiting his contributions in this way, Deep Throat could legitimately claim that he never leaked information. Citing circumstantial evidence, historians have contended that throughout 1972 and early 1973, Deep

The three major television networks devoted somewhat more attention to Watergate than newspapers and news magazines. But their coverage did not have a tremendous impact on American public opinion. In mid-September 1972, for example, a nationwide Gallup Poll revealed that only half the general public had read or heard about Watergate.

The lack of interest in Watergate in the press reflected the inability of Democratic leaders to make Watergate a campaign issue in the weeks leading up to the November 1972 presidential election. Democratic Party leaders repeatedly questioned whether the Watergate affair might eventually uncover corruption in the Nixon White House and re-election campaign. But the Nixon administration and its allies effectively turned aside most of these

Throat believed that the cover-up was limited to Nixon's aides and did not include Nixon himself. Indeed, Deep Throat may have actually been a loyal supporter of the president. He may have been motivated to cooperate with Woodward and Bernstein by a desire to expose the cover-up before it crippled Nixon's presidency. As the reporters themselves stated in *All the President's Men,* Deep Throat "was trying to protect the office [of the presidency], to effect a change in its conduct before all was lost."

After April 30, 1973, however, when Nixon fired many of his closest White House aides, Deep Throat may have reassessed Nixon's involvement in the cover-up. From that point forward, he held only two brief meetings with Woodward. "It was clear that a transformation had come over his friend," concluded Woodward after the first of these meetings. "Deep Throat withdrew from further participation when he realized Nixon had been lying," wrote historian Keith W. Olson in *Watergate.* "No doubt, if this analysis is accurate, Deep Throat regretted his actions because they contributed significantly to Nixon's resignation."

Thirty years after Nixon's resignation, the identity of Deep Throat remains shrouded in mystery. Besides Deep Throat himself, only three other men are believed to know his identity—Woodward, Bernstein, and *Washington Post* executive editor Ben Bradlee. Woodward and Bernstein have vowed to keep his identity a secret until his death or until Deep Throat agrees to make his name known.

charges, painting them as desperate partisan sniping. "In a sense, the White House argued that all the attention to Watergate was no more than electoral strategy, a dirty campaign trick itself on the part of the Democrats," observed historian Michael Schudson in *Watergate in American Memory.*

Nixon Rolls to Easy Re-Election

On November 7, 1972, Nixon cruised to an easy victory over Democratic challenger George McGovern. The president won more than 61 percent of the popular vote and 97 percent of the electoral vote. This landslide triumph reflected not only the American public's doubts about McGovern's candidacy,

Nixon easily defeated Democratic candidate George McGovern in the 1972 presidential election.

but also its perception that the Nixon White House was innocent of wrongdoing in the Watergate affair.

The Nixon administration and Republicans all over the country were delighted by the smashing victory. They claimed that the results gave the president a clear mandate from the American people to pursue his domestic and foreign policy agendas. On February 8, 1973, Nixon confidently told his cabinet and staff at a White House breakfast that "Seventy-three can be and should be the best year ever." But even as he spoke those words, the Watergate cover-up conjured up by the president and his inner circle was slowly falling apart.

Chapter 4

THE INVESTIGATION

People have got to know whether or not their president is a crook. Well, I am not a crook.

– President Richard M. Nixon, May 22, 1973

E ven as the Nixon White House continued to bask in the glow of its lop-sided election victory over Democratic presidential candidate George McGovern, the seven individuals arrested in the Watergate break-in the previous fall learned their legal fate. In January 1973 all five Watergate burglars, as well as the two men who had organized the burglary scheme—G. Gordon Liddy and E. Howard Hunt, Jr.—were found guilty of wiretapping and conspiracy in federal court. Hunt and the four Cuban members of the burglary team pleaded guilty; Liddy and James McCord (the lone non-Cuban member of the burglary team) were convicted by a jury.

Initially, these convictions gave the illusion that the Nixon White House had put the entire messy affair behind it. But in actuality, the trial proceedings indicated that the Nixon presidency remained in jeopardy. Judge John J. Sirica, who presided over the trials of the men, imposed stiff sentences in every case (see Sirica biography, p. 122). But he referred to them as "provisional" sentences, suggesting that he might significantly reduce them if the burglars cooperated with the ongoing FBI investigation into the break-in. Sirica's unusual arrangement reflected a suspicion—held by many people close to the investigation—that the burglars were being paid or pressured by higher authorities in the Nixon campaign to keep silent. "I just didn't believe these people," Sirica later wrote in *To Set the Record Straight*. "The whole case looked more and more like a big cover-up."

U.S. Senate Votes to Open an Investigation into Watergate

On February 7, 1973, the U.S. Senate voted 77-0 to establish a select committee to conduct an investigation of the Watergate affair. The seven-member panel consisted of three Republicans and four Democrats, in accordance with the latter's status as the Senate's majority party. Conservative Democrat Sam J. Ervin of North Carolina was appointed to lead the Senate Select Committee to Investigate Presidential Campaign Practices, which came to be known as the Watergate Committee or the Ervin Committee (see Ervin biography, p. 98).

The White House was alarmed by this new development. White House spokesmen and allies in Congress and the media initially tried to discredit the planned Senate hearings as a partisan witch-hunt. They noted that the Democrat-controlled committee had decided to limit the investigation to Watergate and possible Republican criminal activity during the 1972 campaign, while ignoring Republican concerns about possible campaign abuses and illegal activities carried out by the Democratic Party. The Republican effort to frame the Senate investigation as a politically motivated stunt initially attracted some attention. But the charge slowly faded over time, smothered by a series of dramatic Watergate revelations.

"I just didn't believe these people," Sirica declared. "The whole case looked more and more like a big cover-up."

The first major blow to the cover-up came in early March 1973, during Senate hearings to confirm FBI Acting FBI Director L. Patrick Gray as the next director of the FBI. During the course of these hearings in front of the Senate Judiciary Committee, Gray admitted that he had given White House Counsel John Dean full access to the agency's reports on the Watergate affair. He also acknowledged that he had met with Dean on dozens of occasions to discuss Watergate, and that he had permitted Dean to sit in on FBI interviews of 14 White House aides. These admissions stunned the Senate confirmation panel, angered the Nixon White House, and doomed Gray's nomination. On April 5, Gray finally made a personal request that his name be withdrawn from consideration.

For the previous several months, the *Washington Post* had been virtually the only major news organization to treat Watergate like a major news story (see "Everybody Was Against Us," p. 30). But Gray's statements convinced the national media to take another look at Watergate after months of sporadic coverage. The White House response to the surge in scrutiny was nervous and testy. Press secretary Ron Ziegler's exchanges with reporters inquiring about Watergate became increasingly hostile, and Nixon himself released a blunt statement asserting an extremely broad view of the power of executive privilege (see "Executive Privilege," p. 32).

According to Nixon's interpretation of executive privilege, he was under no legal obligation to share his private conversations with staff to anyone. He insisted that public disclosure of such information could reduce the free exchange of ideas vital to the development of public policy, and that it might also reveal confidential information "harmful to the public interest." The president's interpretation of executive privilege also precluded any of his close aides from testifying about the content of conversations they had with the president. Nixon's declaration irritated the Senate Judiciary Committee, which unanimously voted to "invite" Dean to testify about his relationship with Gray. Dean refused, citing Nixon's stand on the executive privilege issue.

Growing Cracks in the Cover-Up

On March 21, Dean met with Nixon and bluntly warned him that Watergate was "a cancer growing on the presidency." He also warned him that Watergate burglar E. Howard Hunt was extorting CREEP for more money in exchange for his continued silence about "seamy" things he had done on behalf of the White House. But Nixon remained defiant. He signaled his willingness to give Hunt as much as $1 million if necessary, saying "I know where it could be gotten."

One day later, Nixon held a meeting with Haldeman, Ehrlichman, Mitchell, and Dean in which he declared his unwavering commitment to the cover-up plan. "I don't give a shit what happens," he said. "I want you all to stonewall it, let [the burglars] plead the Fifth Amendment, cover-up or anything else, if it'll save the plan. That's the whole point."

On March 23, the cover-up suffered another major blow. On that day, Judge Sirica revealed that Watergate burglar James McCord had decided to cooperate with the court in hopes of receiving a lighter jail sentence. McCord had written Sirica a letter in which he admitted to committing perjury. His letter also disclosed that the Watergate defendants had been under enormous political pressure to keep silent about White House and CREEP involvement in the break-in. Finally, McCord claimed that several people who had been deeply involved in the Watergate operation had not yet been identified by authorities.

"Everybody Was Against Us"

Leonard Downie was one of several editors at the *Washington Post* who worked with Carl Bernstein and Bob Woodward during their investigation of the Watergate scandal. In an interview with author Michael Schudson, published in his 1992 book *Watergate in American Memory: How We Remember, Forget, and Reconstruct the Past,* Downie recalled the tense atmosphere that prevailed in the newspaper's editorial offices, especially during the months when other major news organizations were ignoring the story:

> It was a small group of people against the government.... We felt small. We did not feel big and powerful. We were not swaggering. Our responsibilities were huge to us. We didn't really believe the president was going to resign. Most of us were dysfunctional the night that he resigned because the role which we had played in that looked overwhelming to us. We were very concerned about being right all the time. We were very concerned about the judgments we made. And we were a small group of people. As Ben [Bradlee, executive editor of the *Post*] liked to say, we didn't have subpoena power. We didn't have the FBI. It was a small group of people doing this.... That's still what this business is about. That's still what makes a difference. That's a lesson of Watergate I want to remind people about. It was hard. It was not glamorous at the time. Later on it was glamorous with movies and movie premieres at the Kennedy Center and so on but at the time it was dirty. People weren't sleeping, people weren't showering, Bernstein's desk was a mess, he and Woodward were fighting all the time, they were fighting with their editors all the time, we were all under such great pressure, it was difficult to figure out what was going on because everybody was against us, because people were whispering to Katherine Graham [owner of the *Post*] that they'll ruin her newspaper, and that's still what it's about, you know, initiative and bravery and enterprise. That's what makes a difference.

The release of McCord's letter, combined with Gray's testimony, deeply shook Washington, D.C. Democratic leaders sharpened their charges of a cover-up, and criticism of the Nixon administration intensified within the president's own party. Two Republican senators urged the appointment of an independent prosecutor to investigate Watergate, and another—Lowell Weicker of Connecticut—publicly stated his belief that White House officials had been involved in the break-in.

By this point, many news organizations had become skeptical of White House and CREEP denials of involvement in the Watergate affair. As a result, the Watergate story finally became front-page news in papers beside the *Washington Post* and the *New York Times*. In addition, newspapers, periodicals, and television networks all diverted investigative reporters and other resources to the growing story.

Years later, these reporters would characterize their quest for information as a reasonable effort to unmask corruption at the highest levels of government. In fact, the press's coverage of Watergate is often cited as one of the high points in the history of American journalism. Some of Nixon's allies, however, offered other perspectives on the exploding coverage. Former Nixon speechwriter Raymond Price, for example, claimed that it marked the culmination of years of hostility between Nixon and the news media. "It was the scent of blood—the thrill of the hunt with a quarry they had been after for years," he stated in *Nixon: An Oral History of His Presidency*. "It was a stampede; no one was going to be left behind. The hate was so thick in that town that you couldn't have cut it with a knife."

Dean Decides to Talk

On March 30, McCord gave secret testimony to the Ervin Committee. He revealed that Liddy and Hunt had told him that Nixon's inner circle of advisors—including John Mitchell, John Dean, H.R. Haldeman, Charles Colson, and Jeb Magruder—had all approved or known about the Watergate break-in. A few days later, Dean acted on his growing fear that Nixon and other advisors were setting him up to take the fall for the cover-up. He secretly contacted the Ervin Committee to let them know that he wanted to arrange a deal with prosecutors. He would spill everything he knew about the break-in and cover-up in exchange for consideration at sentencing. (Dean's efforts to exchange his cooperation for outright immunity from prosecution failed.)

Executive Privilege

The concept of "executive privilege" is implied in the U.S. Constitution, and it has been invoked on a number of occasions in the nation's history. It holds that the president—the head of the executive branch of the U.S. government—has the power to keep certain military and diplomatic information secret for the purposes of national security.

As the Watergate scandal intensified, President Nixon embraced a very broad interpretation of the concept of executive privilege. For example, the Nixon White House held that under the doctrine of executive privilege, presidential aides could not be forced to testify before Congress or turn over any of their documents.

Throughout the legal battle over possession of the Watergate tapes, the Nixon administration pinned all of its hopes for keeping the tapes on the concept of executive privilege. It became a key issue of the Watergate scandal, one that would ultimately require the intervention of the Supreme Court to define the limit of the president's right to confidentiality.

On April 15, 1973, Dean informed Nixon that he was talking with the grand jury convened by the Justice Department to investigate Watergate. About this same time, the president learned that both Dean and CREEP Deputy Director Jeb Magruder had implicated top aides Haldeman and Ehrlichman in a number of illegal acts, including the Watergate break-in, destruction of evidence associated with the break-in, and the September 1971 burglary of the office of Daniel Ellsberg's psychiatrist. One of Nixon's main sources of information on these and other aspects of the Justice Department investigation was Assistant Attorney General Henry Peterson, who the president repeatedly pumped for information.

Dean's decision escalated the atmosphere of distrust and self-preservation that now pervaded the White House. It also prompted Nixon, Ehrlichman, and Haldeman—who by this point were the only two advisors the president trusted—to huddle together and hatch a plan to convince Mitchell to take the fall for the whole scandal. Mitchell, however, bluntly refused to sacrifice himself for the president.

The cascade of embarrassing revelations and setbacks left Nixon uncertain how to proceed. He knew that he still enjoyed a fair amount of support from the American public. As recently as April 4, a national Gallup poll found that the president held a solid 60 percent approval rating. But he recognized that Dean's break from the fold and growing evidence that Haldeman and Ehrlichman engaged in criminal activities could quickly erode his standing with the American people.

Even as he pondered what to do about Haldeman, Ehrlichman, and Dean, Nixon reached agreement with the Ervin Committee on the "ground rules" for the testimony of White House personnel. In essence, the president reversed his position regarding testimony by aides, but he maintained the right of executive privilege on specific questions. In announcing this agreement on April 17, Nixon declared that "I condemn any attempts to cover up in this case, no matter who is involved."

Nixon Cleans House

In the closing days of April 1973, Nixon reluctantly concluded that he needed to distance himself from Haldeman, Ehrlichman, and Dean, all of whom were becoming more deeply entangled in the Watergate scandal with each passing day. He pressured all three men into submitting their resignations. During this time he offered emotional apologies to both Haldeman and Ehrlichman, who expressed anger and disappointment with this turn of events.

Nixon also demanded the resignation of Attorney General Richard Kleindienst. The attorney general bitterly objected to the president's order, noting that the timing of his resignation would link him in the public mind to Haldeman, Ehrlichman, and Dean. But the president was determined to secure his resignation. He wanted to announce all four resignations as a symbolic package to the American people, one that would reassure the public that his administration placed a high premium on ethics and trustworthiness. In the end, Kleindienst submitted to Nixon's demand and drew up his resignation.

On April 30, Nixon announced the resignations in a nationwide broadcast from the Oval Office (see "President Nixon Addresses the Nation about the Watergate Investigation," p. 137). This address marked the first time the president spoke directly to the American people about the growing Watergate crisis. "In any organization, the man at the top must bear the responsibility," he declared. "That responsibility, therefore, belongs here, in this office. I accept it. And I pledge to you tonight, from this office, that I will do everything in my power to ensure that the guilty are brought to justice....

> "We must maintain the integrity of the White House, and that integrity must be real, not transparent," stated Nixon. "There can be no whitewash at the White House."

We must maintain the integrity of the White House, and that integrity must be real, not transparent. There can be no whitewash at the White House." Nixon later wrote in his memoirs that his announcement of the resignations left him "so anguished and saddened that from that day on the presidency lost all joy for me."

Haldeman, meanwhile, saw Nixon's decision to oust his closest aides as a major strategic error. "I had a deeply frustrating, useless feeling as the wolves started to close in on the President's heels and as he continued to follow the strategy of throwing an occasional baby to them to try to stop the chase," he wrote in his 1978 memoir *The Ends of Power*. "Unfortunately, each baby, right from the beginning, had only whetted the wolves' appetites and convinced them more strongly that they were on the right track. It was obvious, from the outside, that this was happening, and that in any event he would soon be the last baby left."

Independent Prosecutor Takes Up the Investigation

In the immediate aftermath of Nixon's April 30 speech, the president scrambled to return some semblance of order to his administration. As historian Melvin Small noted in *The Presidency of Richard Nixon*, "Haldeman's and Ehrlichman's forced resignations [had] left the White House in a shambles," and Nixon felt intense pressure to reverse the slide in his administration's fortunes. He promoted Alexander Haig to chief of staff and brought on Leonard Garment as White House counsel. He also turned his attention to the opening in the attorney general's office. Nixon knew that he would have to select a highly respected individual as his administration's new attorney general. Meanwhile, calls intensified in Congress and across the country for the creation of a special prosecutor—who would be selected by the attorney general—to investigate the Watergate affair.

Nixon subsequently nominated Elliot Richardson, an official in his cabinet with a reputation for integrity and reliability, for the position of attorney general. Richardson accepted the post with misgivings, for he knew that the Watergate scandal was a messy situation. But Nixon urged him to take the job, telling him that the attorney general had a duty to get "to the bottom of this" and stating that "you've got to believe I didn't know anything." Almost immediately after his nomination was announced, Richardson signaled his intention to appoint a special prosecutor to investigate Watergate. He also assured the Senate Judiciary Committee during his confirmation hearings that he would give the special prosecutor wide latitude in his investigation.

In May 1973 Richardson announced that Harvard Law School professor Archibald Cox had agreed to serve as special prosecutor. He also stated that Cox would have complete independence to pursue his investigation wherever he saw fit. Publicly, the White House reacted calmly to Cox's selection. Privately, Nixon was deeply angry about the

Archibald Cox was the first special prosecutor to investigate the Watergate scandal.

choice. Cox had been a close associate of John F. Kennedy—who had narrowly defeated Nixon in the 1960 presidential election—and he was a political liberal who had served as solicitor general in the administrations of Democratic presidents Kennedy and Johnson (see Cox biography, p. 87).

Cox tackled the challenges of his new office with gusto. Armed with a generous budget that enabled him to recruit a large number of attorneys and investigators, he did not hesitate in carrying out Richardson's instructions to investigate all possible offenses committed by the Nixon administration—not just those relating to the Watergate break-in and cover up. Nixon later complained in *RN: The Memoirs of Richard Nixon* that "No White House in history could have survived the kind of operation Cox was planning."

The widely held perception that Nixon's White House was under siege became even stronger in May 1973. At that time, a federal judge dismissed charges against Pentagon Paper leakers Daniel Ellsberg and Anthony Russo because of government misconduct during Nixon's first term. Several weeks later, it was revealed that since Nixon had become president, the government had spent millions of dollars of taxpayer funds on his vacation homes at the same time that he had used accounting maneuvers to pay virtually no federal or state income taxes.

Controversy over these revelations festered into the fall, at which time Nixon declared that "I made my mistakes, but in all of my years of public life, I have never profited, never profited from public service—I earned every cent…. People have got to know whether or not their president is a crook. Well, I am not a crook." (In April 1974, the Joint Congressional Committee on Taxation ruled that Nixon owed the IRS $432,787.13 in back taxes, a sum that he never paid in full. Nixon, meanwhile, maintained for the rest of his life that he was not guilty of any wrongdoing on this matter.)

Ervin Committee Begins Public Hearings

On May 17, 1973, the Senate Watergate Committee chaired by Sam Ervin finally began its public Watergate hearings. These hearings continued until August 7. Over this seven-week period, the American public was transfixed by more than 300 hours of televised testimony on network TV. Inevitably, some of the televised hearings were dry and dull. But some of the testimony was truly explosive, and such larger-than-life personalities as Ervin—who projected an aura of folksy resolve—also stoked public interest in the proceedings. "With Ervin at the helm and a galaxy of Nixon aides as witnesses, the Watergate hearings became a spectacle unlike any other political event in the history or this or any other country," confirmed *Washington Post* editor Barry Sussman in *The Great Coverup.*

The hearings went badly for the Nixon administration from the outset. A series of witnesses implicated in the Watergate scandal—including James McCord, Maurice Stans, Jeb Magruder, John Caulfield, and Bernard Barker—gave damaging testimony that deepened public doubts about White House denials of involvement. Desperate to shore up his sagging presidency, Nixon issued a long statement on May 22 in which he repeated his contention that "I took no part in, nor was I aware of, any subsequent efforts that may have been made to cover up Watergate." This statement also included numerous other blatant falsehoods about his involvement in emerging aspects of the scandal. Chief of Staff Alexander Haig, one of the president's most vigorous

Senator Sam Ervin pursued the Watergate investigation with dogged determination.

defenders, later wrote in his book *Inner Circles* that of the seven itemized denials Nixon made in this statement, six were lies.

Media reaction to Nixon's statement, meanwhile, was mixed. The *Los Angeles Herald Examiner*, for example, declared that "Nixon's strong, comprehensive statement ...clearly shows that the President himself was not involved." But the *Wall Street Journal* responded that "the President is acting like a man with something to hide." In any event, Nixon's disclaimer did nothing to slow the investigative efforts of such papers as the *New York Times* and *Washington Post*.

As the public hearings continued, Nixon and the Ervin Committee remained locked in their struggle over possession of White House documents. On July 7 Nixon sent a letter to Ervin in which he firmly stated that he had no intention of handing over presidential papers to the committee. "No President could function if the private papers of his office, prepared by his personal staff, were open to public scrutiny," Nixon wrote in his memoirs. "Formulation of sound public policy requires that the President and his personal staff be able to communicate among themselves in complete candor, and that their tentative judgments, their exploration of alternatives, and their frank comments on issues and personalities at home and abroad remain confidential."

Dean Testimony Rocks the Country

The most dramatic testimony in the televised hearings came from John Dean, who began a full week's appearance before the Ervin Committee on June 25. Before submitting to questions from committee members, Dean read a 245-page statement into the record. During the course of this long mono-logue, he admitted to his central role in the Watergate cover-up. He also stated that Nixon and his closest aides had been actively involved in planning and maintaining the cover-up. Samuel Dash, who served as chief prosecutor for the Ervin Committee, later wrote in *Chief Counsel* that Dean's opening statement "presented a devastating mosaic of intrigue, illegality, and abuse of power participated in by the highest officials in government, including the President of the United States. The worst fears of most Americans, which had been building by speculation, were now realized."

During the question-and-answer phase of his appearance, Dean described a cover-up operation that grew from a seemingly minor bit of polit-ical housekeeping into "a terrible cloud" over the Nixon White House. Throughout his time on the stand, he displayed a composed and articulate manner and a virtual photographic memory. Ervin later described Dean as a "most impressive and convincing witness."

Most importantly, Dean's testimony painted a devastating portrait of the president as a ruthless politician with little respect for the rule of law. "Dean fielded questions adeptly, contradicting the President's versions of events with impressive consistency," wrote Carl Bernstein and Bob Woodward in *The Final Days*. "His story, basically unshakable, held up as an extended accusa-tion against the Nixon White House; wiretapping, burglary, secret funds, money-laundering, enemies' lists, dirty tricks, Plumbers, physical surveil-lance, choreographed character assassination, cover-up, obstruction of the federal agencies."

Republican Senator Howard Baker handled questioning of Dean for the minority. Baker conceded that the former White House counsel's allegations

The testimony of former White House aide John Dean before the Senate Watergate Committee shocked the nation.

were "extraordinarily important" and "mind-boggling." But he observed that much of Dean's information was circumstantial or based on hearsay evidence. With this in mind, Baker pointedly declared that the central question of the hearings was "What did the President know and when did he know it?" As historian Keith W. Olson later wrote in *Watergate,* "By posing this question, Senator Baker intended to protect Nixon, in essence, by forcing investigators to produce specific evidence tying Nixon to the break-in or the cover-up."

Years later, Dean declared in *Nixon: An Oral History of His Presidency* that "I stand on every word of my testimony; I wouldn't retract a word. Do I have some mistaken dates? A few. Given the fact that I had no access to any documents other than newspaper clippings, it's amazing that I didn't miss more. But I wouldn't retract a word of my testimony; I believe it as much today."

Nixon, meanwhile, offered this assessment of Dean's appearance in *RN: The Memoirs of Richard Nixon.* "Dean's testimony was a primer in the dark

H. R. Haldeman flatly denied any White House involvement in the Watergate affair.

underside of White House politics. Thanks to the way he did it, everything was perfectly arranged for the Democrats to distance themselves from their own political past and proclaim that my administration had invented original sin."

Mitchell, Ehrlichman, and Haldeman Testify

After Dean completed his testimony, several other former members of Nixon's inner circle testified before the Watergate committee. Prior to their appearances, all of these aides received coaching and encouragement from Nixon to lie under oath. John Mitchell testified immediately after Dean, and the contrast in attitude from the previous witness was startling to committee members and assembled media alike. "[Mitchell's] recalcitrance, his foggy, vague answers, his angry interruptions, and his snide, sarcastic remarks directed at the committee and at some of his own associates need to be seen and heard to be fully appreciated," wrote Stanley Kutler in *Wars of Watergate*. "His long pauses, his silent rejection of questions, and his facial expressions amply reflected his absolute contempt for the proceedings and his total loyalty to the President."

Haldeman and Ehrlichman also testified before the committee in July 1973. Ehrlichman was a sullen and sarcastic witness who repeatedly contradicted Dean's account of events. Haldeman, meanwhile, adopted a more friendly and conversational tone with committee members. But he flatly denied many of Dean's accusations, and he maintained that both he and Nixon were totally innocent. "President Nixon had no knowledge of or involvement in either the Watergate affair itself or the subsequent efforts of a cover-up of the Watergate," Haldeman declared on July 30. "I had no such knowledge or involvement."

The American public was spellbound by the appearances of Mitchell, Haldeman, and Ehrlichman. But it was the testimony of a lesser-known

White House aide named Alexander Butterfield that ultimately shook the nation to its core. For it was the mild-mannered Butterfield who revealed to the world that Nixon maintained a secret tape recording system in the Oval Office and other areas of the White House. Investigators knew that the contents of these tapes could answer the scandal's central question—"What did the President know and when did he know it?"—once and for all. "The great debate—was John Dean a liar?—could be solved by evidence preserved by the President himself!" marveled Haldeman in *The Ends of Power.*

Chapter 5

THE WATERGATE TAPES

⸺⟆⟇⸺

If Nixon had destroyed the tapes, there would have been no solid, concrete evidence of a cover-up. The tapes were the key evidence that he had participated in obstructing justice. If the tapes had not existed, the situation certainly would have been quite different.

— Former President (and Nixon vice president) Gerald Ford

During John Dean's dramatic testimony before the Senate Watergate Committee chaired by Sam Ervin, he alluded to the possibility of a secret tape recording system in the Oval Office. These remarks prompted committee investigators to ask everyone scheduled to testify before the Ervin Committee if they knew about the existence of such a tape recording system. This questioning extended to so-called "satellite witnesses"—assistants, secretaries, and aides employed by the White House or the Committee to Re-Elect the President (CREEP)—who had been called in by investigators desperate to find someone who could corroborate some of the explosive charges Dean had leveled against the president.

Until July 13, 1973, all witnesses appearing before the Ervin Committee had denied knowledge of any White House tape recording system. On that day, however, White House aide Alexander Butterfield met with investigators from Ervin's Watergate Committee. This interrogation, which was intended to prepare Butterfield for his impending public testimony before the committee, proceeded routinely until the very end. At that time, one of the investigators asked Butterfield if he knew anything about the presence of a tape recording system in the Oval Office. "I was hoping you fellows wouldn't ask that," Butterfield replied.

Butterfield's remark stunned the investigators, who demanded details. Butterfield explained that a taping system had been installed by the Secret Service about 18 months into Nixon's first term. He also told investigators that beside himself, only two other White House aides—former Chief of Staff H. R. Haldeman and his aide Larry Higby—knew of the system's existence. Finally, he revealed that the recording system had been installed not only in the Oval Office, but also in the White House Executive Office Building retreat, the Cabinet Room, several private White House rooms, and the president's cabin at the Camp David presidential retreat in Maryland. "Everything was taped …as long as the President was in attendance. There was not so much as a hint that something should not be taped," Butterfield added.

Investigators later learned that from February 16, 1971, to July 18, 1973—when the recording system was shut down—the system taped approximately 4,000 hours of presidential meetings and telephone conversations. Nixon later confirmed that he installed the system in order to keep a record of his presidency. He had reasoned that the tapes would help him prepare his memoirs after leaving office, and he thought the tapes would be valuable historical artifacts in their own right.

Butterfield revealed the existence of the Nixon tapes to the world on July 16, 1973, when he gave his public testimony before the Ervin Committee. The news triggered a firestorm of reaction. Everyone involved in the Watergate scandal—from the Nixon White House to investigators and reporters—recognized the significance of the tapes: the tapes had the potential to reveal, once and for all, whether Nixon had been truthful when he said that he was not involved in the Watergate cover-up. One day after Butterfield's testimony, on July 17, 1973, Ervin formally asked the White House to release the tapes to his committee. Special Prosecutor Archibald Cox, who was carrying out a separate investigation of the Watergate affair, made a similar request on July 18.

Nixon pondered this new development from a hospital bed, where he was being treated for a serious case of viral pneumonia. Aides and advisors huddled around his bedside to discuss how the president should respond to the tape requests. Many people urged the president to destroy the tapes, insisting that they were private property that he could dispose of in any way he pleased. But White House counsel Leonard Garment threatened to resign and go public with his objections if this "evidence" was destroyed. More importantly, Nixon himself was convinced that the tapes could not legally be taken from him, so he decided not to destroy them.

Alexander Butterfield's testimony about the secret White House taping system stunned the Ervin Committee.

Nixon's decision to keep the tapes instead of destroying them remains one of the great points of debate of the Watergate scandal. As historian Stanley Kutler wrote in *The Wars of Watergate,* "of the numerous imponderables about Watergate, Nixon's failure to destroy the White House tapes is one of the most bewildering and confusing." Many observers admit that destroying the tapes would have triggered widespread condemnation. But they also speculate that, with the tapes gone, Nixon could have survived any impeachment proceedings.

Years later, Nixon himself recalled his decision to keep the tapes with enormous regret and bitterness. "If I had indeed been the knowing Watergate conspirator that I was charged as being," he declared in *RN: The Memoirs of Richard Nixon.* "I would have recognized in 1973 that the tapes contained conversations that would be fatally damaging. I would have seen that if I were to survive they would have to be destroyed."

Constitutional Showdown

After consultating with his advisors, Nixon formally turned down both requests for the White House tapes. The president insisted that the tapes were private property. In addition, he claimed that their contents were "entirely consistent with what I know to be the truth and what I have stated to be the truth." Nixon also repeated his claim that turning over the tapes would be a dangerous violation of the principle of executive privilege. Finally, he asserted that the tapes contained material that could compromise national security.

The president's refusal to release the tapes to Ervin and Cox was harshly criticized by investigators. It also proved to be a public-relations disaster with the American people, who voiced growing doubts about the president's integrity and truthfulness. Nixon was battered by charges that he was purposely hindering the investigation into the Watergate affair, and his approval ratings declined dramatically.

Unwilling to take no for an answer, both the Ervin Committee and Cox asked Watergate trial judge John Sirica to issue subpoenas for several of the tapes. (A subpoena is a judicial order that compels the recipient to testify or provide evidence in legal proceedings.) In the case of the Ervin Committee, it voted unanimously to call for the subpoenas. This marked the first time since 1807 that a congressional committee had subpoenaed a president (in 1807 President Thomas Jefferson was subpoenaed to testify at the treason trial of former Vice President Aaron Burr; Jefferson declined to appear, establishing an early precedent for the concept of executive privilege).

On August 29, Sirica ordered the president to give him the tapes for his own private review. The judge hoped that this compromise would satisfy Nixon's desire to protect presidential privacy while also upholding the principle that the courts had ultimate authority over defining what material qualified for protection under the executive privilege doctrine. But the Nixon White House refused to recognize the subpoenas, stating that the president was under no legal obligation to turn over the tapes. This stance paved the way for a momentous constitutional showdown between Congress and the presidency. Both sides clearly felt that the law was on their side.

Angered by Nixon's stand, the Ervin Committee promptly asked the courts to force Nixon to obey the subpoenas. The fundamental issue, Ervin later wrote in *The Whole Truth,* was "whether the President is immune from all of the duties and responsibilities in matters of this kind which devolve upon all the other mortals who dwell in this land." Special Prosecutor Cox joined in the battle as well, insisting that the White House had no legal right to withhold the tapes. In early September, Sirica ruled that he did not have the power to force the president to release the tapes. But this ruling was only a modest victory for the Nixon administration, since it merely moved the battle over possession of the tapes to a higher court, the U.S. District Court of Appeals.

Nixon Fires Cox

On October 12, 1973, the U.S. District Court of Appeals ordered Nixon to turn over the subpoenaed Watergate tapes. Cox and Ervin expressed satisfaction with the decision, but they knew that Nixon and his lawyers might challenge the ruling. Initially, however, the administration held off on filing an appeal of the court's decision. Instead, the White House countered with a compromise that it said would relieve the "constitutional tensions of Watergate." It offered to release edited transcripts of the tapes, but under strict terms. Under the proposal, Nixon would provide a summary of the tapes' contents under the supervision of Democratic Senator John Stennis of Mississippi. In return for this concession, Nixon wanted Cox to "make no further attempts by judicial process to obtain tapes, notes or memoranda of presidential conversations." Nixon also reminded Cox that his status as an employee of the executive branch made him subject to the directives of the Oval Office.

> *"I am certainly not out to get the president of the United States," Cox said "I am even worried, to put it in colloquial terms, that I am getting too big for my britches."*

Nixon and his advisors hoped that their strategy would neutralize Cox, or even convince him to resign. But Cox refused to back down. Instead, he mounted a public relations offensive that received widespread coverage on television and in print. Cox condemned the administration for noncompliance with the court order, and he reminded the country that he had been guaranteed total independence in pursuing his investigation. "I am certainly not out to get the president of the United States," Cox said in a nationally televised press conference. "I am even worried, to put it in colloquial terms, that I am getting too big for my britches, that what I see as principle could be vanity. I hope not. In the end I decided that I had to try to stick by what I thought was right."

Former U.S. Attorney General Elliot Richardson was fired by Nixon when he refused to fire Special Prosecutor Cox.

Cox's refusal to obey Nixon's directive gave the White House a clear-cut excuse to fire him. On October 20, 1973, Nixon called Attorney General Elliot Richardson into the Oval Office. The president ordered Richardson, who was Cox's direct superior, to fire the special prosecutor. But Richardson flatly refused. Instead, he reminded the president that Cox had been promised total independence in his investigation. When Nixon refused to relent, Richardson regretfully submitted his own resignation. Angered and distressed by Richardson's stand, Nixon lashed out. "I'm sorry that you insist on putting your personal commitments ahead of the public interest," declared the president. Richardson replied defiantly, stating "I can only say that I believe my resignation *is* in the public interest."

After Richardson's departure, Nixon ordered Deputy Attorney General William Ruckelshaus to fire Cox. But Ruckelshaus refused as well, and he submitted his resignation a short time later. Nixon and his aides then turned to Solicitor General Robert Bork, who dismissed Cox effective immediately. Cox left, but not before issuing a brief public statement in which he mused that "whether we shall continue to be a government of laws and not of men is for Congress and ultimately the American people" to decide.

Years later, Cox acknowledged that he knew his clashes with Nixon had placed his job in jeopardy. "I suppose if anyone had said to me, 'Won't the result of this be that you will be fired?' I would have responded, 'I guess so,'" he told Gerald and Deborah Hart Strober in *Nixon: An Oral History of His Presidency.*

> I truly think this was not important in my mind at the time. The most important thing was that the rule of law should prevail; the president must comply with the law. This depends whether the people in a moral and political sense will rise up and force

The Saturday Night Massacre escalated anti-Nixon sentiment across the country and prompted demonstrations outside the White House.

him to comply with the law. Will they understand what is at stake? Because, ultimately, all their liberties were at stake.

The White House under Siege

In the immediate aftermath of Cox's ouster, a wave of relief washed over the White House. Nixon and his inner circle convinced themselves that the events of October 20 had rid the administration of a dangerous foe (Cox) and tightened the president's grip on the tapes. But the White House completely underestimated media and public reaction to the departures of Cox, Richardson, and Ruckelshaus.

The American public expressed outrage over the firings and resignations, which came to be known collectively as the "Saturday Night Massacre." In homes, businesses, and universities across the country, anger and dismay at the president's actions reached a new high. *Newsweek* magazine described

49

the furious reaction as "a nationwide rebuke" that constituted "the most devastating assault that any American president has endured in a century."

In the days following the White House shake-up, Nixon's approval rating with American voters plummeted to an astounding 17 percent, according to a national Gallup poll. This decline in public confidence reflected a fundamental and dramatic reassessment of the Watergate affair by legislators and ordinary Americans alike. Prior to the Saturday Night Massacre, most people did not think that the scandal posed a mortal threat to the Nixon presidency. But afterward, the terms "impeachment" and "resignation" popped up much more frequently in public discourse.

Indeed, over the space of two days (October 23 and 24) following the Saturday Night Massacre, 44 Watergate-related bills were introduced in the U.S. Congress. Fully half of these bills called for an impeachment investigation. (In the impeachment process, the House of Representatives decides whether an indictment of the president for criminal wrongdoing is justified. If the House makes such a determination, the chief justice of the Supreme Court presides over a trial, with the Senate serving as jury. If the president is found guilty of "high crimes or misdemeanors," he is removed from office.)

"President Nixon is impeaching himself in the minds and hearts of his countrymen," warned the **Dallas Times Herald.**

The change in the public mood was also evident on the nation's editorial pages. Several leading newspapers and magazines boldly called for Nixon to step down. The *Dallas Times Herald,* for example, declared on October 22 that "President Nixon is impeaching himself in the minds and hearts of his countrymen." *Time* magazine suspended its policy of never writing editorials in order to publish one that called for Nixon's resignation in extremely strong terms (see "*Time* Magazine Urges Nixon to Resign," p. 147).

Even staunch defenders of the president changed their positions. The editors of the *Salt Lake Tribune* stated on October 22, 1973, that "In view of our years of support for the man and for many of his policies, we regret that we now find it necessary, for the good of the country, to call upon Richard M. Nixon to resign." And newspapers that chose not to call for Nixon's resignation still issued blistering editorials about his perceived lack of integrity and principles. "We have reached a point where we no longer can believe our President," lamented the *New Orleans State-Item.*

The scale and intensity of the negative reaction sent the White House reeling. As it struggled to respond, Nixon and his advisors came to the unwelcome realization that the president's choices to fill the attorney general and special prosecutor vacancies could not be perceived as being even mildly friendly to the administration. The president subsequently selected William Saxbe as attorney general and Leon Jaworski as special prosecutor (see Jaworski biography, p. 105). The choice of Jaworski was viewed with some skepticism by some members of Congress and a number of staffers in the Special Prosecutor's Office. The mere fact that the White House had selected him cast a shadow over his

Leon Jaworski succeeded Cox as Special Prosecutor in the Watergate case.

appointment. But as soon as Jaworski and Saxbe assumed their duties, it became clear that they intended to pursue the Watergate investigation with the same aggressive tenacity as their predecessors.

The Deadlock Continues

As October 1973 drew to a close, the tapes remained in Nixon's possession. But both sides realized that the legal battle over them would ultimately be decided by the United States Supreme Court. In the meantime, the Nixon White House suffered further blows to its credibility. On October 10, 1973, Vice President Spiro Agnew became the first vice president in U.S. history to resign because of criminal charges. These charges—bribery, extortion, and tax fraud—were unrelated to the Watergate affair, but they cast another stain on the tattered reputation of the Nixon administration. In the meantime, the Internal Revenue Service's ongoing investigation into Nixon's tax records continued to generate negative headlines.

Then, in November 1973, the White House abruptly claimed that two of the subpoenaed tapes did not even exist. It also admitted that another one of the subpoenaed tapes contained a mysterious 18½ minute gap. Nixon's secretary, Rose Mary Woods, claimed that she had accidentally erased part of the tape. But her explanation was widely dismissed, and administration critics pointed to the erasures as clear evidence that Nixon could not be trusted with the tapes. (On January 15, 1974, a panel of six technical experts reported that the gap was the result of five separate manual erasures.) By December 1973 Chairman Sam Ervin had become convinced, as he later wrote in his memoirs, that Nixon's sole reason for keeping the tapes was "to hide … the truth respecting Watergate."

In December 1973, Michigan Congressman Gerald R. Ford took the oath of office as the country's new vice president, succeeding Agnew. Ford was selected over other potential candidates because of his strong loyalty to the Republican Party and his solid public reputation. The Ford nomination sailed easily through both Senate and House confirmation votes, and he was sworn in on December 6.

Sirica Listens to the Tapes

A few days later, the White House finally turned the subpoenaed tapes over to Judge Sirica. Joined by his young law clerk, Sirica carefully listened to the tapes (see "Judge Sirica Listens to the First Wave of Watergate Tapes," p. 152). In his memoir *To Set the Record Straight,* Sirica acknowledged that the tapes convinced him that "we did have a dishonest man in the White House, a president who had violated the law, who had conspired to obstruct the very laws he was sworn to uphold. It was a frightening thing to know." After listening to all the tapes, Sirica upheld claims of executive privilege or irrelevance on all or parts of three tapes, then turned the remaining tapes over to Special Prosecutor Jaworski and the grand jury.

When Jaworski listened to the tapes, he felt sure that they proved that Nixon had been criminally involved in the Watergate cover-up. His staff of investigative lawyers agreed. But in a remarkable display of restraint and professionalism, they never leaked the contents of the tapes to the news media. Instead, they debated how to proceed against a sitting president who had apparently committed crimes while holding office.

On January 9, 1974, the Watergate prosecutors signaled their determination to press forward when Jaworski requested more White House tapes. Fearful of negative reaction from Congress and the American public, Nixon and his inner circle did not officially deny the request. But they engaged in a pattern of stalling tactics to keep them out of Jaworski's hands.

On January 30, 1974, Nixon delivered the annual State of the Union address to the nation. He spent most of the speech highlighting his administration's accomplishments over the previous five years. But he also took advantage of the spotlight to declare that "one year of Watergate is enough." Finally, he signaled his determination to fight his accusers to the bitter end, vowing that he had "no intention whatever of ever walking away from the job that the people elected me to do for the people of the United States."

Nixon's words did nothing to calm public opinion. Instead, the ongoing battle for possession of the tapes kept the nation in turmoil. In addition, the legal struggles of dozens of individuals caught up in the investigation of the Watergate break-in and cover-up were widely reported by the press, which contributed to the uproar. "Relentlessly, week after week, investigations, indictments, confessions, trials, charges, and countercharges were reported, whether by the print media or by radio and television," stated historian Keith W. Olson in *Watergate*. "The legal processes in a democracy are complex and time-consuming, and with the president involved, the public had a right to know about each procedural step. And the public seemed interested."

In December 1973 Judge John Sirica finally received the first of the subpoenaed White House tapes.

Washington Post managing editor Ben Bradlee put the level of public interest in Watergate in even stronger terms. "No news story has ever grabbed and held Washington by the throat the way Watergate did," he recalled in a June 14, 1992, column in the *Post*. "No news story in my experience ever dominated conversation, newspapers, radio and television broadcasts the way Watergate did. There were times when you could walk whole city blocks and ride taxis all around town and never miss a word of hearings or press conferences."

Nixon's Options Dwindle

On February 6, 1974, the House of Representatives voted by a 410-4 tally to launch a formal impeachment inquiry. Three weeks later, the House

Judiciary Committee asked Nixon to turn over another group of tape recordings. This development greatly concerned Nixon, for unlike the Special Prosecutor's Office, the House had a clear constitutional right to carry out impeachment proceedings against the president. The administration stalled for time, reluctant to refuse the request outright.

In the meantime, Nixon's political fortunes continued to slide. In mid-March, prominent Republican Senator James Buckley of New York publicly called for Nixon's resignation. According to Buckley, Americans had lost faith in the president's "credibility and moral authority." He also argued that Nixon's troubles constituted a major threat to the institution of the presidency. Buckley's remarks reflected widespread concern within the Republican Party over Nixon's actions and their impact on the party.

On March 1 Special Prosecutor Jaworski secured indictments for obstruction of justice from the federal grand jury against seven Nixon aides. The grand jury also named Nixon as an "unindicted co-conspirator," meaning that Nixon would not be indicted by legal authorities, but he was considered a conspirator in the criminal actions. This action reflected Jaworski's belief that a sitting president was not subject to criminal indictment by a grand jury. Nixon's new status as an unindicted co-conspirator was not revealed to the American public, however.

Desperate to turn the tide of public opinion and avoid a confrontation with the House Judiciary Committee, Nixon released a 1,300-page transcript of the Watergate tapes on April 29, 1974. Upon releasing the edited transcripts, he admitted that some of the material in the transcripts was embarrassing. But he insisted that the material would show that he had no prior knowledge of the Watergate break-in until March 21, 1973, when he met with former White House Counsel John Dean.

As investigators combed through the details of the documents, ordinary Americans expressed shock at the profanity, racist remarks, and naked political calculations that dotted the transcript. "It is difficult after listening to the tapes or reading the transcripts to emerge with much admiration for Richard Nixon as a person," wrote historian Melvin Small in *The Presidency of Richard Nixon*:

> Nixon's defenders contend that one should not take literally
> much of what he said on the tapes; he was merely blowing off
> steam and thinking out loud, as demonstrated by the fact that
> many of his orders were not carried out. But some of those

Under enormous political pressure, President Nixon released edited transcripts of White House tapes—the so-called "blue books"—in April 1974.

orders were carried out, and saying that he was merely blow-
ing off steam does not excuse the racial and religious slurs that
littered his conversations.

Lawmakers from both parties expressed displeasure over the contents of
the transcripts. In fact, historian Stanley Kutler notes in *The Wars of Watergate*
that some of the harshest reactions came from Republicans. Senator Hugh
Scott described the transcripts as "shabby, disgusting, immoral," and Senator
Robert Packwood expressed amazement that Nixon did not voice "even any
token clichés about what is good for the people." The "overall flavor" of the
transcripts, concluded Kutler, "devastated [Nixon's] public standing and left
him naked to the winds of criticism. The October firestorm [the Saturday
Night Massacre] left burning embers; the release of the tape transcripts in
April and May rekindled the flames. It was another disaster."

The Supreme Court Decision

President Nixon relied on the concept of executive privilege in his legal battle to retain control over the tapes of his White House meetings and conversations. But on July 24, 1974, the U.S. Supreme Court unanimously ruled that President Nixon had to release the tapes and turn them over to investigators.

In its opinion in *U.S. v. Nixon,* the Supreme Court agreed that the office of the president had some constitutionally based rights to confidentiality. But it stated that since Nixon's claim of executive privilege was based "solely on the broad, undifferentiated claim of public interest in the confidentiality of [presidential] conversations, a confrontation with other values arises." The Court ruled that the privilege of confidentiality did not outweigh the legal system's need to gather important evidence in deciding criminal cases. The Court also expressed deep concern that Nixon's interpretation of executive privilege would upset the balance of power among the three branches of the U.S. government—the executive, legislative, and judicial branches. The Court feared that if Nixon's interpretation of executive privilege had been allowed to stand, it would have crippled the U.S. Congress's lawful right to investigate wrongdoing in the executive branch.

On July 8, 1974, the battle for possession of the subpoenaed Nixon tapes finally reached the U.S. Supreme Court. Justice William Rehnquist recused himself because he had worked under Nixon in the Justice Department many years earlier. The other eight justices listened as Special Prosecutor Leon Jaworski and White House Counsel James St. Clair presented their cases. On July 24, the Supreme Court issued a unanimous decision that Nixon was legally obligated to turn over all of the subpoenaed tapes (see "The Supreme Court Decision," p. 56).

When Nixon learned of the Supreme Court's decision, he sensed that his political career was nearly over. After all, one of the tapes contained the record of his conversation with former Chief of Staff H. R. Haldeman on June 23, 1972, when Nixon had clearly stated his approval of a cover-up of the

Many observers believe that when the Supreme Court considered the case, it made a special effort to come up with a unanimous decision. In an interview for *Nixon: An Oral History of His Presidency,* former assistant attorney general William Ruckelshaus explained the importance of this goal:

> On a lot of decisions that involve issues of national moment, the Court strives mightily to come out with a unanimous decision. They used to do it in civil rights cases and, particularly where they are making new law which has an impact on the country, they try very hard to come up with unanimous decisions; they recognize that any dissent on the Court would divide the country and provide ammunition for those who oppose the decision and, thereby, keep the country in sort of an ambiguous position relating to those kinds of policy. I thought they would decide [the tapes issue] unanimously.... As the president became weaker, and as his actions—particularly where he became involved in the discharge of myself, Elliot Richardson, and Archibald Cox—gave the impression, at least, that he was trying to hide something, it became more likely that they would be released. The Supreme Court is not immune to the strength of public support, or nonsupport, for the president or the congressional branch.

Watergate break-in. The contents of this tape were conclusive proof—the so-called "smoking gun" sought by Watergate investigators—that Nixon had been deeply involved in the cover-up within days of the Watergate burglary.

Nixon Turns Over the Tapes

On July 24, 1974, the House Judiciary Committee concluded its investigation and prepared to vote on whether to recommend impeachment (see "Representative Barbara Jordan's Speech on Constitutional Law, July 25, 1974," p. 156) On July 27, 1974, the House Judiciary Committee passed its first article of impeachment by a 27-11 vote, sending the article to the full House for a vote. This was soon followed by two other articles of impeachment accusing Nixon of obstructing justice in the Watergate affair (see "House Judiciary Committee Resolution to Impeach President Nixon," p. 161).

Throughout the proceedings, the members of the House Judiciary Committee went about their business in a careful, methodical manner. Each step of the way, the committee took great care to make sure that Americans understood the impeachment process. This somber and serious approach proved reassuring to the American public. "Whatever one's sentiments about impeachment, the prevailing view was that the televised proceedings had conveyed an image of congressional conscientiousness, intelligence, and fair-mindedness," observed Kutler. "Those images nourished a public confidence that lent some legitimacy and calm to the eventual outcome of events."

> *"We can be lied to only so many times," said Senator Barry Goldwater. "The best thing [Nixon] can do for the country is to get the hell out of the White House, and get out this afternoon."*

On August 2, Republican representative Charles Wiggins, who had long been the administration's fiercest advocate on the committee, went to the White House. At Nixon's invitation, he read the transcript of the June 23 tape. After reading the transcript, though, Wiggins urged the president to release the tape. He also warned Nixon that the contents of the tape meant certain impeachment and conviction.

Over the weekend of August 3 and 4, Nixon huddled with family, aides, and members of Congress to ponder his next step. He received conflicting advice in these meetings. Members of his immediate family, for example, urged him to stand firm and fight impeachment. His wife and daughters had been steadfastly loyal to Nixon throughout the Watergate ordeal, and they were extremely distraught at the thought of seeing him resign the presidency. But many other advisors and friends pleaded with him to resign for the good of himself, his family, and the nation.

On August 5, 1974, Nixon released all the subpoenaed tapes, including the "smoking gun" tape of June 23, 1972. At the same time, he issued a public statement acknowledging that "portions of the tapes of these June 23 conversations are at variance with certain of my previous statements." The last remnants of Nixon's defenses collapsed with the release of the tapes. Representative Wiggins, for example, publicly announced "with great reluctance and deep personal sorrow [that] I am prepared to conclude that the magnificent career of public service of Richard Nixon must be terminated." Republican Senator Barry Goldwater was more blunt. "We can't support this any longer. We can be lied to only so many times. The best thing he can do for the country is to get the hell out of the White House, and get out this afternoon."

The overwhelming negative reaction to the tapes finally forced Nixon to concede that his presidency was doomed. There was no doubt that if he refused to resign, he would be removed from office. He thus began making preparations to inform the nation that he was ready to bring his troubled presidency to a close.

Chapter 6

NIXON'S RESIGNATION AND PARDON

◄━━ɪɪɪɪʃɪɪɪɪ━━►

I let the American people down, and I have to carry that burden with me for the rest of my life.

–President Richard M. Nixon on August 8, 1974, the day
before he resigned the presidency

The contents of the tapes that President Nixon released on August 5, 1974, sealed his fate. Most importantly, the tapes confirmed his deep involvement in the Watergate cover-up and exposed his many lies about the affair. But the tapes also revealed that Nixon conducted daily business in the Oval Office in a manner that millions of Americans found morally offensive.

With the release of the Watergate tapes, the American public braced itself for the resignation that was almost certain to come. "The news is bombarding us again, and one has no choice but to receive it, to stay by the radio and the phone," wrote journalist Elizabeth Drew in *Washington Journal*. "Events are hurtling forward, and all one can do is try to keep up."

To be sure, small bands of diehard Nixon supporters continued to gather outside the White House. In addition, a few lawmakers vowed to support the president to the bitter end. The most famous of these individuals was Earl Landgrebe, a Republican congressman from Indiana. "Don't confuse me with the facts," he declared during a television appearance. "I won't vote impeachment ...not even if they take me outside and shoot me."

But Landgrebe's was a lonesome voice, even among Republicans. On August 6 every Republican member of the House Judiciary Committee stated their intention to vote in favor of impeaching Nixon. Beside Landgrebe, only

Crowds gathered outside the White House gates on the morning of Nixon's resignation.

one other member of the 435-member U.S. House of Representatives publicly indicated that he would vote against impeachment.

Nixon Announces His Resignation

On Tuesday, August 6, Nixon began penning a resignation speech. As he struggled with the unpleasant task, he told Chief of Staff Alexander Haig and White House Press Secretary Ron Ziegler that he had decided to resign Friday and announce it Thursday night. "Well, I screwed it up real good, didn't I?" Nixon told them.

As the week progressed, some supporters and family members urged Nixon to stay in office and fight impeachment (see "The Speech Nixon Never Gave," p. 64). But he recognized that such a stand would only prolong his agony, for he had virtually no support in the nation's capital or around the country. On August 7 he spoke by telephone with former Chief of Staff H. R.

Nixon announced his intention to resign the presidency in a nationally televised address to the nation.

Haldeman, who urged him to consider a blanket pardon for all the Watergate defendants, but Nixon was noncommittal. Later that evening the president met in the White House residence quarters with Secretary of State Henry Kissinger, who had helped him register his administration's most significant foreign policy triumphs. Nixon later described the meeting as a warm reminiscence of their years working together. Kissinger, though, wrote that Nixon acted like a man who had been "shattered" by the events of Watergate.

On the morning of August 8 Nixon notified Vice President Gerald Ford of his decision to resign effective at noon the following day. Later that evening, he met with congressional leaders to confirm that he intended to resign. By the end of the meeting, Nixon was in tears.

At 9:00 P.M. eastern time, Nixon began his nationally televised resignation speech, speaking through the camera to a dazed and spellbound nation

The Speech Nixon Never Gave

As the Watergate scandal unfolded, presidential speechwriter Raymond Price prepared a speech for Nixon in the event that the president decided to face impeachment rather than resign. The speech was first published as "A President's Non-Resignation Address: The Watergate Words Never Spoken" in the *New York Times* on December 22, 1996. It admits that the president made mistakes, but insists that they were not serious enough to warrant his removal from office. Following are excerpts from the speech, which was never shown to Nixon:

> When I reviewed the June 23 tape, and realized the interpretations that will probably be placed on it, I seriously considered resigning.... If I were to resign, it would spare the country additional months consumed with the ordeal of a Presidential impeachment and trial.

> But it would leave unresolved the questions that have already cost the country so much in anguish, division, and uncertainty. More important, it would leave a permanent crack in our Constitutional structure: it would establish the principle that under pressure, a President could be removed from office by means short of those provided by the Constitution. By establishing that principle, it would invite such pressures on every future President who might, for whatever reason, fall into a period of unpopularity....

(see "President Nixon's Resignation Speech," p. 166). He declared that quitting the office of the president ran counter to his every instinct, but that he felt that his departure would be the best thing for the country. "Therefore, I shall resign the Presidency effective at noon tomorrow," he declared.

As he continued his speech, Nixon never fully owned up to the tapestry of lies and deceit that he had created during the two-year Watergate crisis. But he expressed hope that his departure would open a new and more hopeful chapter in the nation's history. "I regret deeply any injuries that may have been done in the course of the events that led to this decision," he stated. "I would say only that if some of my judgments were wrong—and some were wrong—they were made in what I believed at the time to be the best interest of the nation."

For me to see this through will have costs for the country in the short run. The months ahead will not be easy for any of us. But in the long run—whatever the outcome—the results will be a more stable form of government. Far more damaging than the ordeal of a Senate trial, far more damaging than even the conviction and removal of a President, would be the descent toward chaos if Presidents could be removed short of impeachment and trial.

Throughout the Western world, governmental instability has reached almost epidemic proportions.... In the United States, within the last dozen years one President was assassinated; the next was in effect driven from office when he did not even seek re-election; and now the third stands on the verge of impeachment by the House of Representatives, confronted with calls for his resignation in order to make the process of removal easy.

This country bears enormous responsibilities to itself and to the world. If we are to meet those responsibilities in this and future Presidencies, we must not let this office be destroyed—or let it fall such easy prey to those who would exult in the breaking of the President that the game becomes a national habit. Therefore, I shall see the Constitutional process through—whatever its outcome.

Many close aides and family members had expressed concern that Nixon might not be able to get through the address without breaking down. To their great relief, he kept his composure throughout the speech. Afterward, however, Nixon was shaky and bathed in sweat.

Reactions to the Resignation

Across most of America, the overwhelming reaction to Nixon's resignation speech was one of palpable relief. The spectacle of Watergate had been undeniably fascinating to millions of Americans, but the affair had also been profoundly frightening, disillusioning, and emotionally exhausting. Americans viewed Nixon's departure and Ford's move into the Oval Office as an opportunity to put the scandal behind them and begin the healing process.

George McGovern, who lost to Nixon in the 1972 presidential election, acknowledged that he was surprised at the speed with which Nixon resigned after handing over the tapes. "I don't remember being bloodthirsty myself," he told Gerald and Deborah Hart Strober in an interview for *Nixon: An Oral History of His Presidency*. "I had every reason to be, but I don't recall saying much about it one way or the other. I thought the House did a very good job in the way they handled it, and I think if it had come to a vote in the Senate, the Senate would have voted with the House, probably enough so that it would have been a clear decision. My guess is that the Senate would have gone along with it somewhat reluctantly. I am sure in Nixon's mind he saw resignation as the least painful and degrading way to handle a rather unhappy situation."

Nixon's Last Hours as President

On the morning of August 9, Nixon assembled his family and selected White House and administration workers for what he called a "spontaneous" speech of appreciation (*see* President Nixon's Parting Remarks, p. 171). Setting aside the protests of his family, he permitted television cameras into the room. He then launched into a long and rambling monologue that sometimes seemed directed more at future generations of Americans than the people in the room. "I let the American people down, and I have to carry that burden with me for the rest of my life," he admitted. He also devoted several minutes to praise for his mother and father. Finally, he dispensed several nuggets of advice—such as "those who hate you don't win unless you hate them, and then you destroy yourself"—that sounded jarring coming from a man whose political career had been brought down by ruthless and vengeful political maneuvers.

Nixon and his wife Pat then flew by helicopter to Andrews Air Force Base, where they boarded the plane that would take them back to their home in California. After the doors closed and the plane lifted off, silence descended on the passenger cabin. "There was no talk, there were no tears left," explained Nixon in *RN: The Memoirs of Richard Nixon*. "I leaned my head back against the seat and closed my eyes. I heard Pat saying to no one in particular, 'It's so sad. It's so sad.'"

Back at the White House, meanwhile, Gerald Ford was sworn in as the 38th president of the United States at 12:03 p.m. eastern time. Ford thus

Nixon hugs his youngest daughter Julie shortly after delivering his resignation. At left are Nixon's oldest daughter Tricia and his son-in-law Ed Cox.

became the first president in U.S. history never to have won a vote as a candidate for vice president *or* president. In his first public remarks as president, Ford declared, "My fellow Americans, our long national nightmare is over."

Ford Pardons Nixon

After Nixon's resignation, the American public and its elected representatives were divided on whether to pursue criminal charges against the ex-president. Many people believed that Nixon's humiliating resignation was punishment enough and that he could never get a fair trial. But many others asserted that he should be subject to the same criminal justice system as any other American.

The Watergate Special Prosecution Force headed by Special Prosecutor Leon Jaworski acknowledged the belief in some quarters that Nixon had suffered enough, but it nonetheless signaled its intention to proceed with its

Nixon gives the "V for victory" salute to White House staff members in the waning moments of his presidency.

Gerald Ford was sworn in as the 38th president of the United States at noon, August 9, 1974.

prosecution of Nixon. After all, the prosecution and sentencing of other figures implicated in the Watergate scandal continued without pause in the weeks following Nixon's resignation (see "Key Figures of Watergate—Legal Charges and Jail Sentences," p. 70).

Nonetheless, Ford felt increasing pressure from his party to pardon Nixon so that Republicans—and the country as a whole—could finally put the Watergate mess behind them once and for all. If Nixon was prosecuted, warned White House Counsel Leonard Garment, "the whole miserable tragedy will be played out to God knows what ugly and wounding conclusion." This argument resonated with Ford, who later stated in his memoir *A Time to Heal* that he felt growing certainty that "the hate had to be drained and the healing begun."

On September 8, 1974, Ford signed Proclamation 4311 granting "a full, free, and absolute pardon unto Richard Nixon for all offenses against the United States, which he, Richard Nixon, had committed or may have com-

Key Figures of Watergate— Legal Charges and Jail Sentences

Following is a rundown of the legal charges and jail sentences of key figures associated with the Watergate affair.

Nixon, Richard M. – Unindicted co-conspirator; pardoned by President Gerald Ford.

Barker, Bernard – Pleaded guilty to conspiracy, burglary, wiretapping, and unlawful possession of surveillance devices; sentenced to 18 months to 6 years in prison; served 12 months before gaining release.

Chapin, Dwight L. – Convicted of lying to a grand jury; sentenced to 10-30 months in prison; served 8 months before release.

Colson, Charles "Chuck" W. – Pleaded guilty to obstruction of justice; sentenced to 1-3 years in prison and fined $5,000; served 7 months.

Dean, John W., III — Pleaded guilty to conspiracy to obstruct justice; sentenced to 1-4 years in prison; served 4 months.

Ehrlichman, John D. – Convicted of perjury, conspiracy to violate civil rights, and conspiracy to obstruct justice; sentenced to concurrent terms of 20 months to 8 years in prison; served 18 months before release.

Gonzalez, Virgilio R. – Pleaded guilty to conspiracy, burglary, wiretapping, and unlawful possession of surveillance equipment; sentenced to 1-4 years in prison; served 15 months before release.

Haldeman, H.R. – Convicted of perjury and conspiracy to obstruct justice; sentenced to 30 months to 8 years in prison; served 18 months before release.

Hunt, E. Howard – Pleaded guilty to conspiracy, burglary, and wiretapping; sentenced to 30 months to 8 years in prison, as well as a $10,000 fine; served 33 months before release.

Kalmbach, Herbert – Pleaded guilty to violation of the Federal Corrupt Practices Act and to promising federal employment in return for political activity; sentenced to $10,000 fine and 6-18 months in prison; served 6 months.

Kleindienst, Richard G. – Pleaded guilty to refusal to answer questions of Senate subcommittee; sentenced to 30 days in jail and $100 fine; sentence was later suspended.

Krogh, Egil, Jr. – Pleaded guilty to conspiracy to violate civil rights; served more than 4 months of 2-6 year sentence (all but 6 months of sentence were suspended).

LaRue, Frederick – Pleaded guilty to conspiracy to obstruct justice; served more than 5 months of 1-3 year sentence (all but 6 months of sentence were suspended).

Liddy, G. Gordon – Convicted of conspiracy, conspiracy to violate civil rights, wiretapping, and burglary; sentenced to serve 6 years and 8 months to 20 years in prison, as well as $40,000 fine; Liddy ultimately served 52 months in prison, the longest period of incarceration for any Watergate figure.

Magruder, Jeb – Pleaded guilty to conspiracy to obstruct justice, wiretapping, and fraud; sentenced to 10 months to 4 years in prison; released after 7 months.

Martinez, Eugenio R. – Pleaded guilty to conspiracy, burglary, wiretapping, and unlawful possession of surveillance equipment; convicted of conspiracy to violate civil rights; served 15 months of 1-4 year prison sentence.

McCord, James W., Jr. – Convicted of conspiracy, burglary, wiretapping, and unlawful possession of surveillance equipment; served 4 months of 1-5 year prison sentence.

Mitchell, John N. – Convicted of conspiracy to obstruct justice and perjury; served 19 months of 30-month to 8-year prison sentence.

Segretti, Donald H. – Pleaded guilty to violations of campaign law and conspiracy; served more than 4 months of 6-month prison sentence.

Stans, Maurice H. – Pleaded guilty to five misdemeanor violations of the Federal Elections Campaign Act; fined $5,000.

Sturgis, Frank W.` – Pleaded guilty to burglary, conspiracy, wiretapping, and unlawful possession of surveillance equipment; served 13 months of 1-4 year prison sentence.

mitted or taken part in during the period from January 20, 1969 through August 9, 1974." Nixon responded with a statement of acceptance (see "President Ford's Statement Pardoning Nixon, and Nixon's Statement in Response," p. 176). Later, in his memoirs, Ford expressed unhappiness with Nixon's response to the pardon. "[His statement] hadn't been as forthcoming as I had hoped," Ford wrote. "He didn't admit guilt and it was a good deal less than a full confession."

Ford's decision to pardon Nixon proved enormously unpopular with the American people. As Ford himself later wrote *A Time to Heal,* the American public "wanted to see him drawn and quartered publicly." In the days following his issuance of the pardon, the public goodwill that Ford enjoyed in the weeks following his ascent to the presidency evaporated. His favorability ratings in polls dropped from 71 percent to 49 percent, and countless editorials fumed that the pardon enabled Nixon to escape the full measure of punishment he deserved. Republican leaders, meanwhile, expressed dismay with the timing of the pardon, as it came only three months before the 1974 Congressional elections. They recognized that American voters would punish Republican politicians for Ford's pardon.

The outcry about the pardon rocked the Ford administration, as did persistent (and unsubstantiated) rumors that Nixon had only resigned in exchange for a guarantee that he would receive a full pardon in return. Determined to address the issue squarely, Ford took the unusual step of volunteering to explain his decision before a House Judiciary subcommittee. His appearance in mid-October 1974 marked the first time a president had testified in Congress since George Washington's presidency.

Ford's decision to pardon Nixon proved politically fatal. In the 1976 presidential election, Ford lost the popular vote to Democratic Party nominee Jimmy Carter by 2 percent. Exit polls revealed that 7 percent of voters had voted against Ford solely because of his decision to issue the Nixon pardon.

Years later, some people continue to believe that the pardon was a terrible mistake. "I said at the time—and continue to think—the pardon violated the principle that all individuals, powerful and powerless, rich and poor, must stand equally at the bar of justice after they are charged with criminal wrongdoing," stated former Watergate Special Prosecutor Archibald Cox in *Nixon: An Oral History of His Presidency.* "He was excused from that." As the years have passed, however, perceptions of Ford's decision to pardon his predecessor have changed somewhat. Many historians, political leaders, and ordinary citizens now say that Ford's decision to pardon Nixon was a wise and selfless decision that spared the nation a great deal of heartache and pain.

Chapter 7

THE LEGACY
OF WATERGATE

━━◅⊲◖∿◗⊳▻━━

> Our greatest possession is not the vast domain; it's not our
> beautiful mountains, or our fertile prairies, or our magnifi-
> cent coastline.... These things are of great importance. But in
> my judgment the greatest and most precious possession of
> the American people is the Constitution.
>
> > –Sam Ervin, in a commencement address at
> > Davidson College in North Carolina

In the years since the Watergate affair spilled onto American television screens and newspapers, American politicians, journalists, historians, and ordinary citizens have offered differing perspectives on the scandal's legacy. Many would concur with historian Stanley Kutler, who in *The Wars of Watergate* described Watergate as "the nation's most sustained political conflict and severest constitutional crisis since the Great Depression," while others have seen it as an affirmation of the nation's founding principles.

Advocates of this position believe that the painful affair ultimately confirmed the strength of the U.S. political system and underscored the wisdom of the nation's Founding Fathers. These men, after all, were the creators of a Constitution that emphasized the sharing of political power— and rejected the idea that any man or woman was immune from the laws that governed the rest of society. "When President Nixon was untrue to his constitutional obligations, Congress and the federal judiciary remained true to theirs," declared Sam Ervin in *The Whole Truth*. "As a consequence, the United States weathered a great national crisis without turmoil and with all its institutions intact."

But others have interpreted the Watergate affair as a cautionary event in American history. They acknowledge that "the system worked" in that the criminal actions surrounding Watergate were uncovered and punished. But as former Vice President Walter Mondale wrote in *The Accountability of Power: Toward a Responsible Presidency,* "Our system worked, but it worked only with the aid of a good deal of luck and a great deal of hard work.... Good fortune alone will not preserve a democracy in which there is no will to guard against the abuse of power."

> *"Our system worked, but it worked only with the aid of a good deal of luck and a great deal of hard work,"* remarked Walter Mondale. *"Good fortune alone will not preserve a democracy in which there is no will to guard against the abuse of power."*

Indeed, President Richard Nixon's resignation stemmed from a series of fateful events that had a cumulative impact far exceeding their individual significance. These events included the fortuitous discovery of the burglars' activities, the selection of Judge John Sirica to hear the burglary case, the providential assignment of reporters Bob Woodward and Carl Bernstein to the story, John Dean's fateful decision to turn against Nixon, the steady hand of Senate Watergate Committee Chairman Sam Ervin, the resolve of Watergate prosecutors Archibald Cox and Leon Jaworski, and—most of all—the lucky discovery that Nixon had a secret tape recording system in his offices. The point that Mondale and many others make is that if any single element of this convergence of events had not occurred, the Watergate investigation might have stalled. And Richard Nixon would have served out his full second term without ever being called to account for his criminal activities.

Watergate's Impact on Nixon's Legacy

In the years following Watergate, many people associated with the affair, from Nixon's inner circle of aides to the prosecutors and reporters who brought the scandal to light, have offered their own interpretations of Watergate events. Many of these memoirs and interviews contained new accusations or conspiracy theories about the scandal, as well as rationalizations about their criminal conduct. Other figures implicated in Watergate crimes accepted responsibility for their actions or at least made a genuine effort to explain the reasons for the things they did.

Of all the Watergate figures, however, no one made a greater effort to rehabilitate himself in the eyes of the American people than Nixon himself. Nixon's deep concern about his presidency's place in history led him to write a series of books on foreign affairs and other subjects and to consciously project an image of himself as a wise elder statesman of American politics.

Nixon's strategy worked, to some degree. He received sympathetic coverage from major news outlets in the years immediately prior to his death in 1994, and his funeral triggered an outpouring of statements praising his service to America (see "Senator Dole's Comments at Nixon's Funeral," p. 80). The passage of time also prompted many politicians, government officials, and scholars to look beyond Watergate to other aspects of his presidency. "The substantive actions of the Nixon administration will be viewed with great regard, particularly in foreign policy," asserted Nixon Secretary of Defense James Schlesinger in *Nixon: An Oral History of His Presidency* by Gerald and Deborah Hart Strober.

Nixon spoke out on many issues during his post-Watergate years.

But Nixon's efforts to burnish his historical reputation fell short with many other Americans. Writing in his 1988 memoir, Republican Senator Barry Goldwater displayed his still-intense anger at Nixon's actions, declaring that "he was the most dishonest individual I ever met in my life. President Nixon lied to his wife, his family, his friends, long-time colleagues in the U.S. Congress, lifetime members of his own political party, the American people, and the world." And historian Stanley Kutler, writing in *The Wars of Watergate,* bluntly stated that

> Nixon cannot escape his history. Despite various 'comebacks' and 'recoveries' since 1974, he has been unable to shake loose from the Watergate quagmire. For it is Watergate and the unprecedented spectacle of a presidential resignation that dis-

Nixon (second from left) was joined by two former presidents—Ronald Reagan (left) and Gerald Ford (right)—and President George H. W. Bush (second from right) for the 1990 opening of his presidential library in Yorba Linda, California.

tinguish Nixon's uniqueness and significance in American history. Watergate remains his burden and his legacy…. History will record a fair share of the significant achievements of Nixon's presidency, but Watergate will be the spot that will not out.

Watergate's Impact on American Journalism

The Watergate crisis also has had a tremendous impact on the shape and character of American journalism. In fact, media scholar Larry Sabato claimed in his book *Feeding Frenzy* that Watergate has "had the most profound impact of any modern event on the manner and substance of the press's conduct."

In the view of Sabato and many other observers, the drama of Watergate—and the press's role in exposing elements of the scandal—moved American journalists to adopt a much more aggressive and skeptical attitude toward

The Watergate reporting of Bob Woodward (left) and Carl Bernstein (right), seen here in a 1998 appearance on "Meet the Press," altered the face of American journalism.

American government and other institutions. "The story of Bob Woodward and Carl Bernstein in bold pursuit of the perpetrators of the Watergate break-in is resonant and powerful in both the world of journalism and the culture at large," wrote Michael Schudson in *Watergate in American Memory,* referring to the Woodward-Bernstein book *All the President's Men* and the resulting film.

> The film, even more than the book, ennobled investigative reporting and made of journalists modern heroes…. Journalists do remember Watergate; whether they lived through it or not, "Watergate" holds a place in their understanding of what their job is and what it might be, what the significance of their work is and what it might be. What is most important to journalism is not the spate of investigative reporting or the recoil from it after Watergate but the renewal, reinvigoration, and remythologization of muckraking. The muckraking theme has been powerful in American

Senator Dole's Comments at Nixon's Funeral

Former president Richard Nixon died on April 22, 1994, in New York City. On April 27, a funeral service for Nixon was held in Yorba Linda, California. Attendees included President Bill Clinton and all four living ex-presidents. The service was marked by a number of speakers who praised Nixon's life and presidency, including Republican Senator Bob Dole. Following are excerpts from Dole's comments:

> I believe the second half of the 20th century will be known as the age of Nixon. Why was he the most durable public figure of our time? Not because he gave the most eloquent speeches, but because he provided the most effective leadership. Not because he won every battle, but because he always embodied the deepest feelings of the people he led.
>
> One of his biographers said that Richard Nixon was one of us. And so he was. He was a boy who heard the train whistle in the night and dreamed of all the distant places that lay at the end of the track. How American. He was a grocer's son who got ahead by working harder and longer than everyone else. How American....
>
> To tens of millions of his countrymen, Richard Nixon was an American hero, a hero who shared and honored their belief in working hard, worshipping God, loving their families and saluting the flag. He called them the silent majority. Like them, they valued accomplishment more than ideology. They wanted their government to do the decent thing, but not to bankrupt them in the process.
>
> They wanted his protection in a dangerous world, but they also wanted creative statesmanship in achieving a

journalism for a century, even though its practice is the exception, not the rule. It is hard work. It is painstaking. It is expensive. It is often unrewarding. It runs against the ideological grain of professional neutrality.... Woodward and Bernstein did not simply renew, they extended the power of the muckraking image.

genuine peace with honor. These were the people from whom he had come and who have come to Yorba Linda these past few days by the tens of thousands—no longer silent in their grief. The American people love a fighter. And in Dick Nixon, they found a gallant one.

It is true that no one knew the world better than Richard Nixon. And as a result, the man who was born in a house his father built would go on to become this century's greatest architect of peace. But we should also not underestimate President Nixon's domestic achievements. For it was Richard Nixon who ended the draft, strengthened environmental and nutritional programs, and committed the government to a war on cancer. He leapfrogged the conventional wisdom to propose revolutionary solutions to health care and welfare reform, anticipating by a full generation the debates now raging on Capitol Hill....

Today our grief is shared by millions of people the world over, but it is also mingled with intense pride in a great patriot who never gave up and who never gave in. To know the secret of Richard Nixon's relationship with the American people, you need only listen to his own words: "You must never be satisfied with success," he told us, "and you should never be discouraged by failure. Failure can be sad, but the greatest sadness is not to try and fail, but to fail to try. In the end, what matters is that you have always lived life to the hilt."

Strong, brave, unafraid of controversy, unyielding in his convictions, living every day of his life to the hilt, the largest figure of our time whose influence will be timeless—that was Richard Nixon. How American. May God bless Richard Nixon and may God bless the United States.

However, many people fear that in the years since Watergate, the press's zeal to uncover scandal has produced a downturn in the quality of American journalism. Certainly, numerous news organizations endeavor to offer balanced and insightful coverage of political events, issues, and figures in the United States. But many others fall far short in these regards. And while a Watergatefueled appetite for scandal is cited as one of the major factors in the shortcomings of modern American journalism, it is not solely to blame. Another factor cited is the explosive growth of 24-hour Internet and cable news coverage, which has been blamed for creating a feverish news-gathering environment. The consolidation of media outlets into the ownership of a few large corporations, meanwhile, has prompted fears that censorship of stories that are critical of corporate behavior is on the rise. Finally, many observers believe that political leaders and interest groups have become more sophisticated at manipulating the press and "spinning" news stories to advance their own causes.

When mixed together, these individual factors can have a particularly detrimental effect. During the 1990s, for example, media critic Steven Brill charged in the essay "Pressgate" that in reporting such controversies as the Monica Lewinsky scandal, which threatened the presidency of Bill Clinton, the press often "careened from one badly sourced scoop to another in an ever more desperate need to feed its multimedia, 24-hour appetite." As a result, said Brill, the "press has abandoned its treasured role as a skeptical 'fourth estate.'"

Former Watergate assistant prosecutor Richard Ben-Veniste sees much of today's political coverage as hysterical and invasive, with an emphasis on titillating scandal over substantive examination of public policy. "Whether it is the creeping tabloidization of America, or changes in the economics of the news business, or simply an instinct for pack journalism, there appears to be a decline in critical judgment used to evaluate the importance of a story," he commented in a 1997 column for the *Houston Chronicle*. "Rather than seeing the media as pro-conservative or pro-liberal, pro-Republican or pro-Democrat, I see today's journalists as profoundly and uncritically pro-scandal."

Other observers are less critical, but even they admit that the quality of American journalism varies widely. "There has been a Dickensian quality to investigative reporting and the American press since Watergate," wrote critic Douglass K. Daniel in *The Big Chill*. "A mixture of the best of times and the worst of times. Great stories and embarrassing errors. New media that brought promise and problems."

Watergate's Impact on American Politics and Culture

Watergate's long-term influence on American politics and culture has also been a subject of great debate. In the immediate aftermath of Watergate,

A Writer Laments Lost Lessons of Watergate

In 2002 numerous U.S. news organizations took advantage of the 30th anniversary of the Watergate break-in to revisit the crisis it triggered. They also took the opportunity to assess the scandal's continuing legacy on American politics and culture. Some commentators argued that the Watergate scandal had strengthened the nation's foundations. Others emphasized their belief that Watergate unfairly obscured significant contributions that President Richard Nixon made to his country. But others reached the same conclusion as columnist Richard Reeves, who expressed deep anger and dismay about Watergate's fading place in the American consciousness. "The real story and lessons of Watergate are in peril of being lost or forgotten," he declared in "Assessing Watergate 30 Years Later," which appeared in the June 30, 2002, edition of the *New York Times*.

> Thirty years of research, scholarship and confession—millions of documents, thousands of tapes—have made it perfectly clear that the botched break-in of June 17, 1972, at the Democratic National Committee offices was actually a small incident in Nixon's deliberate, if sometimes clumsy, effort to secretly create a new kind of all-powerful presidential government that reflected his own contempt for democracy and for the Constitution's checks and balances designed to restrict the power of presidents.... There will always be political scandal revealed in a country with a healthy free press. But Watergate was unique as the climax of a presidency that believed that governance required lies and deception. Though Nixon was pardoned, his legacy was the destruction of American faith in government and its elected leaders. And that—not the heroics of the press—is what should be remembered about the episode called Watergate.

lawmakers, political commentators, and ordinary Americans all expressed fears that one likely legacy of the scandal would be a decline in American trust and respect for its governmental institutions and political leaders. This fear has been borne out, thanks in part to political controversies and scandals in subsequent administrations.

Yet many observers also expressed hope that the scandal would usher in a new era of ethical and moral conduct in the nation's political and social institutions. The Watergate affair did prompt a score of legislative reforms designed to prevent future Watergates from ever happening. These included the Budget and Impoundment Control Act of 1974; the 1978 Ethics in Government Act, which provided for the appointment of an independent counsel to investigate White House misdeeds; the 1974 amendment to the Federal Election Campaign Act; the 1974 and 1978 Presidential Materials and Preservation Acts; and a multitude of reforms to the CIA and FBI. These measures were passed for the specific purpose of making governmental and political operations more open to public scrutiny.

By the early 1980s, though, many people remained unconvinced that Watergate had had any beneficial effect on American governance or morality. Writing in 1982 in *Lost Honor,* John Dean declared that "post-Watergate morality" was dead, and he insisted that "it is clear that Watergate has had no lasting effect, has brought no real changes in government, and has had little impact on the people of the country."

During the 1980s and 1990s, many observers expressed concern that the lessons of Watergate were fading from public memory altogether. Historian Joan Hoff-Wilson lamented to *U.S. News and World Report* that Watergate was a dim and distant curiosity to undergraduate students, and she openly wondered whether the scandal would come to be seen as an insignificant event in American history. In a 1986 national survey of high school students compiled by Diane Ravitch and Chester Finn called *What Do Our 17-Year-Olds Know?*, more than one in three students did not know that Watergate took place after 1950. More than one in five students associated the scandal with the resignation of a president other than Nixon.

Even figures closely associated with the Watergate affair acknowledged that the importance of the events of that era did not seem to be fully appreciated. "I am not sure that historians in the next century who were not there will understand the turmoil the country was in during the Watergate period," admitted former President Gerald Ford in 1994 in *Nixon: An Oral History of His Presidency.* "I don't think 30 years from now, that anybody who goes back and reads things will understand the intensity—and the controversy—that exists. If you weren't there, you don't understand it."

BIOGRAPHIES

Archibald Cox (1912-2004)
First Watergate Special Prosecutor

Fired by Nixon White House in the Infamous "Saturday Night Massacre"

Archibald Cox was born on May 17, 1912, in Plainfield, New Jersey. He was one of six children born to Archibald and Frances Bruen (Perkins) Cox. He spent his childhood in Plainfield, then moved on to Harvard University as an undergraduate student in 1930. His arrival on the Harvard campus marked the beginning of a long and rewarding relationship with the school.

Cox earned a bachelor's degree in American history and economics in 1934, then enrolled in the Harvard Law School, where he was a top performer in both the classroom and on the staff of the *Harvard Law Review*. He earned his law degree in 1937, and later that year gained entry to the Massachusetts bar.

After a brief stint as a law clerk in New York, Cox moved on to the private sector with a Boston law firm. In 1937 he married Phyllis Ames, with whom he eventually raised three children. In 1941 Cox joined the staff of the National Defense Mediation Board, then quickly moved over to a position with the Department of Justice's Office of the Solicitor General.

By the end of World War II Cox was working in the Department of Labor as counsel to Labor Secretary Frances Perkins. At war's end, he returned to Harvard Law School as a lecturer. Within one year he was promoted to professor, becoming one of the youngest faculty members in the school's history. He spent the next 15 years at Harvard, where he burnished a reputation as one of the country's leading law scholars.

Cox's tenure at Harvard was interrupted by several periods of public service. During these forays, accomplished through leaves of absence, Cox worked on a wide range of labor issues. By the late 1950s he had emerged as an important advisor to Democratic Senator John F. Kennedy. He played a particularly important part in shaping Kennedy's views on labor issues during this period.

Cox worked energetically on Kennedy's successful 1960 presidential campaign. When Kennedy became president he named Cox as solicitor general, the official who represents the federal government in cases argued before the U.S. Supreme Court. He served as solicitor general from 1961 to 1965, during which time he presented arguments before the Court on civil rights and other major issues of the day. He then returned to the faculty of Harvard Law School.

Appointed Head of the Watergate Special Prosecution Force

Like the rest of America, Cox watched the unfolding Watergate scandal with considerable interest. In May 1973 Attorney General Elliot Richardson—who had been one of Cox's students at Harvard many years earlier—announced his intention to appoint a special prosecutor to investigate the Watergate affair.

Richardson approached several highly regarded members of the legal profession, but was turned down. When he approached Cox, however, the Harvard professor indicated strong immediate interest. After receiving assurances that he would be given complete independence in his investigation, Cox accepted the offer on May 18, 1973, and he took his oath one week later.

Cox launched a vigorous investigation that dismayed President Richard Nixon and the White House. Already suspicious of Cox because of his ties to Kennedy, they watched unhappily as Cox assembled a staff of lawyers and investigators that was larger than all but six of the 94 U.S. Attorneys' offices across the country.

Over the next several months, Cox and the Nixon White House clashed on multiple occasions, in increasingly public fashion. Most of these battles centered on possession of tape recordings of conversations that had taken place between Nixon and various aides in the Oval Office and other areas of the White House. The existence of these tapes was revealed in mid-July 1973, and from that point forward Watergate investigators (both Cox's Special Prosecution Force and the Senate Watergate Committee) engaged in a tense struggle with Nixon for those tapes.

When Cox learned of the existence of the White House taping system, he immediately subpoenaed several of the tapes. The Senate Watergate Committee chaired by Sam Ervin took a similar step. They were rebuffed by Nixon, who claimed executive privilege. Cox appealed in the courts, and on

August 29, 1973, Judge John Sirica ordered Nixon to release the subpoenaed tapes to him so that he could determine if the president's claim of executive privilege was legitimate. Nixon still refused, but on October 12, 1973, the U.S. Court of Appeals upheld Sirica's decision to enforce Cox's subpoena.

Desperate to keep the tapes, Nixon offered a "compromise" measure in which he would give Cox summaries of the taped conversations in return for an agreement not to subpoena any additional White House tapes, documents, and memoranda. "Immense pressure was put on Cox to accept—pressure of a kind hard for outsiders to appreciate," wrote James Doyle, an aide with the Watergate Special Prosecution Force, in *Not Above the Law*. "He was operating on his own, without a political base, without advice beyond that of his young staff, and he could not be sure that holding out was the right thing for the country. But his commitment was to the law, and he rejected the attempt to bypass it."

Cox Holds Out for the Tapes

After rejecting Nixon's offer, Cox signaled his determination to force the president to heed the rule of law. He issued a statement on October 19 declaring that

> In my judgment, the President is refusing to comply with the court's decree. A summary of the content of the tapes lacks the evidentiary value of the tapes themselves. No steps are being taken to turn over the important notes, memoranda and other documents that the court orders require. I shall bring these points to the attention of the court and abide by its decision. The instructions [of the President directing Cox not to seek further tapes, notes or memoranda of presidential conversations] are in violation of the promises which the Attorney General made to the Senate when his nomination was confirmed. For me to comply with those instructions would violate my solemn pledge to the Senate and the country to invoke judicial process to challenge exaggerated claims of executive privilege. I shall not violate my promise....

By this time, rumors were rampant that Nixon was on the verge of firing Cox—whose office was technically part of the Executive Branch and thus under Nixon's authority—for his continued pursuit of the tapes. On October

20 Cox held a press conference in which he acknowledged the possibility. He admitted that Richardson might fire him if Nixon gave him a direct order. "Eventually a president can always work his will," he said. "You remember when Andrew Jackson wanted to take the deposits from the Bank of the United States and his treasury secretary said he could not do it, he fired him; then he appointed a new secretary of the treasury and he would not do it so he fired him; and finally he got a third who would. That is one way of proceeding."

But Cox spent most of the press conference explaining the legal bases for his stand and assuring the American people that he was not acting out of any personal animosity toward the president. "I read in one of the newspapers this morning the headline 'Cox Defiant,' Cox stated. "I don't *feel* defiant. In fact I told my wife this morning I hate a fight. Some things I feel very deeply about are at stake, and I hope that I can explain and defend them steadfastly." According to observers, Cox did an excellent job of laying out his position. Historian Stanley Kutler, for example, wrote in *The Wars of Watergate* that Cox "offered a masterful professorial performance, designed to explain the legal and constitutional confrontation in terms that struck at the core of layman's treasured values essential to the American system."

The "Saturday Night Massacre"

Later that day Nixon ordered Richardson to fire Cox. Richardson refused and submitted his resignation instead. Deputy Attorney General William Ruckelshaus also resigned rather than dismiss Cox. Finally, Solicitor General Robert Bork carried out Nixon's instructions and fired Cox.

These events, dubbed the "Saturday Night Massacre" by the national media, shocked and outraged the American public. Support for Nixon in Congress and in American living rooms plummeted, and the president never really recovered. He eventually was forced to turn over the Watergate tapes, and in August 1974 he became the first president in U.S. history to resign from office.

After his dismissal, Cox returned to Harvard. He served as Williston Professor of Law until 1976, Carl M. Loeb University Professor from 1976 to 1984, and as professor emeritus beginning in 1984. Cox also remained heavily involved in social and political causes. In 1980 he was named chair of Common Cause, a national citizens' advocacy group, and he held that position for the next dozen years. Cox also wrote numerous books on labor law and the American legal system, including *The Role of the Supreme Court in American Government* (1976), *Freedom of Expression* (1981), and *The Court and the Constitution* (1987). He died at his home in Brooksville, Maine, on May 29, 2004.

Sources

Doyle, James. *Not Above the Law: The Battles of Watergate Prosecutors Cox and Jaworski*. New York: William Morrow, 1977.

Gormley, Ken. *Archibald Cox: Conscience of a Nation*. Reading, MA: Addison-Wesley, 1997.

Jaworski, Leon. *The Right and the Power: The Prosecution of Watergate*. New York: Reader's Digest Press, 1976.

Kutler, Stanley. *The Wars of Watergate: The Last Crisis of Richard Nixon*. New York: Knopf, 1990.

John Dean (1938-)
White House Counsel to President Nixon

Provided Testimony Explicitly Linking Nixon to the Watergate Cover-Up

John Wesley Dean III was born on October 14, 1938, in Akron, Ohio. His parents were John Wesley Dean, a businessman, and Sara (Magill) Dean. After graduating from Staunton Military Academy in Virginia, Dean attended Colgate University (1957-59) and Wooster College in Ohio, where he graduated with a bachelor's degree in 1961. In February of the following year he married Karla Ann Hennings, daughter of Missouri Senator Tom Hennings. In 1965 Dean graduated from Georgetown University in Washington, D.C., with a law degree.

After leaving Georgetown, Dean quickly lined up a job with the law firm of Welch and Morgan. He left six months later under controversial circumstances. During the Watergate hearings it was alleged that Dean had been dismissed because of "unethical conduct." Both parties later described his departure as stemming from a "disagreement" over company policies, but the incident left an ethical cloud over the young lawyer.

In any event, Dean was not out of a job for long. In 1966 he was hired as chief minority counsel to the House Judiciary Committee of the U.S. House of Representatives. At that time Republicans were the minority party in the House of Representatives, so over the ensuing months he became acquainted with many Republican lawmakers, aides, and supporters. He gained a reputation around the nation's capital during this time as a loyal, ambitious, and smart staff member.

In 1967 Dean moved on to take a position as associate director of the National Commission on Reform of Criminal Law. During his tenure there he actively supported the presidential candidacy of Richard M. Nixon. When Nixon won the White House in November 1968, Dean's efforts were rewarded with a job as assistant in the Office of the U.S. Attorney General. In 1970 his first marriage ended in divorce.

Counsel to the President

In June 1970 Dean accepted a surprise offer to become general counsel to the president. Other government officials expressed surprise that Dean had been given the job, given his relative inexperience. But the White House supposedly wanted a "good soldier" in the position who would do as he was told, and Nixon's aides decided that Dean was a good choice.

At first, Dean had little contact with Nixon or his top aides. Instead, he spent his days overseeing a small staff of lawyers that handled a wide range of routine legal matters for the president. Over time, however, Dean's responsibilities broadened to include more important tasks—including a role as the compiler of intelligence reports on the activities of antiwar activists.

On October 13, 1972, he married Maureen Kane, with whom he had one son. By this time, Dean had risen to a position of prominence in the White House. He was not quite a member of Nixon's innermost circle of aides, which was led by Chief of Staff H. R. Haldeman and Advisor John Ehrlichman. But he was accepted by Haldeman and other top staffers, who appreciated Dean's apparent willingness to carry out any task for the Republican cause. For example, the ambitious young attorney became deeply involved in the Nixon White House's campaigns against antiwar activists, Democratic Party leaders, and other "enemies" of the Nixon administration. As part of this effort, Dean helped plan the spring 1972 Watergate break-in and cover-up that toppled the Nixon presidency two years later.

When the Watergate scandal erupted, Dean took a leading role in the cover-up of links between the burglars and the White House and Nixon's re-election campaign. He arranged bribes for the arrested Watergate burglars in an effort to buy their silence, leaked confidential information gathered by investigators to Nixon allies, and coordinated the various alibis and lies used by the White House and the Committee to Re-Elect the President (CREEP) to keep investigators from finding the truth. Dean's efforts soon made him a regular visitor to Nixon's Oval Office.

At first, Dean's pleasure at having penetrated Nixon's inner circle overwhelmed all his other feelings. But as the Watergate scandal dragged on, he became despondent and frightened about his deep involvement in the cover-up. On March 21, 1973, he met with Nixon and told the president everything he knew about the cover-up. He also warned Nixon that Watergate constituted a "cancer" that threatened his presidency. "At the end of the meeting I was disappointed," Dean later told Gerald Strober and Deborah Hart Strober in *Nixon: An Oral History of His Presidency.* "I knew we had big trouble. If you listen to my voice on the tape, I'm pretty down by the end of the meeting. I hadn't tried to distort, but I tried to put the most serious consequence picture on everything. I tried to paint it as black as I could without painting it blacker than it should be, and I'd failed.... I failed because Richard Nixon wanted the cover-up to go on. He'd been in it from day one."

Dean's Testimony Shocks America

On April 30, 1973, Nixon fired Dean. By this time, Dean had already decided to cooperate with federal investigators. In June 1973 he delivered four days of nationally televised testimony before the Senate Watergate Committee. His sensational testimony not only revealed Nixon's involvement in the Watergate cover-up, but also cast a harsh light on a wide range of other illegal activities in which the Nixon White House had engaged.

The White House and its allies responded to Dean's damaging appearance with harsh denunciations of his character and motives. They characterized Dean as the rogue mastermind of the Watergate conspiracy and insisted that his testimony had been laced with lies and false statements. Several years later, in fact, Nixon declared in *RN: The Memoirs of Richard Nixon* that Dean's Watergate testimony was "an artful blend of truth and untruth, of possible sincere misunderstandings and clearly conscious distortions. In an effort to mitigate his own role, he transplanted his own total knowledge of the cover-up and his own anxiety onto the words and actions of others." In reality, however, none of Dean's stunning revelations about illegal White House activities were untrue. In fact, most of the damning charges in Dean's testimony were confirmed by the Watergate tapes a few months later.

In October 1973, Dean pleaded guilty to obstructing justice in the Watergate investigation. On September 3, 1974, he began serving a one-to-four-year prison sentence, but spent only four months incarcerated before Judge John Sirica reduced his punishment to time served. While serving his brief sentence, Dean testified for the prosecution in the trials of several other Watergate figures, including John Ehrlichman, John Mitchell, and H. R. Haldeman.

Upon gaining his release from prison, Dean wrote a memoir about Watergate called *Blind Ambition.* The book's publication in 1976 attracted a great deal of public attention. Reviewers seized upon the occasion to condemn Dean for his actions in the White House, but they also acknowledged that the work was a lively and interesting insider's account of the scandal. In 1982 he published a second book, *Lost Honor*, in which he reflected on the state of American politics and his own post-Watergate experiences.

In recent years Dean has divided his time between writing, investment banking, and occasional commentary on government affairs and Watergate-related issues for cable news networks.

Sources

Dean, John. *Blind Ambition: The White House Years.* New York: Simon & Schuster, 1976.

Dean, John. *Lost Honor.* Los Angeles: Stratford Press, 1982.

Dean, Maureen, and Hays Gorey. *Mo: A Woman's View of Watergate.* New York: Simon & Schuster, 1975.

Nixon, Richard. *RN: The Memoirs of Richard Nixon.* New York: Grosset & Dunlap, 1978.

Strober, Gerald S., and Deborah Hart Strober, eds. *Nixon: An Oral History of His Presidency.* New York: HarperCollins, 1994.

John Ehrlichman 1925-1999
Domestic Policy Advisor to President Richard Nixon

Central Figure in the Watergate Cover-Up

Born in Tacoma, Washington, on March 20, 1925, John D. Ehrlichman was a decorated Air Force pilot during World War II. After the war he attended UCLA, where he met H. R. Haldeman for the first time. After graduating in 1948, he enrolled at Stanford Law School, earning a law degree in 1951. He then practiced law privately, rising to the position of partner in a Seattle law firm. In 1968 he was an important campaign manager for the Nixon presidential campaign, and after Nixon took office he brought Ehrlichman with him to the White House.

Ehrlichman was officially known first as President Nixon's White House counsel and then as his chief advisor for domestic affairs. But his "off the books" responsibilities included directing the White House's "plumbers unit" that carried out many illegal schemes, including the Watergate break-in. After Nixon decided to cover up his administration's involvement in the burglary, he relied heavily on both Ehrlichman and Haldeman for advice and reassurance. Indeed, the two aides were deeply involved in the Watergate cover-up from the outset.

White House efforts to put the Watergate burglary story to rest ultimately failed. Instead, multiple investigations gradually uncovered the administration's efforts to deceive Congress and the American public. Speculation about the complicity of Haldeman and Ehrlichman in the affair grew with each passing week. At the height of the Watergate investigation, the names "Haldeman" and "Ehrlichman" seemed virtually inseparable in news accounts of the unfolding scandal. As a result, Ehrlichman resigned from his White House post on April 30, 1973, under pressure from Nixon. Haldeman submitted his resignation the same day.

Even after Nixon's August 1974 resignation, Watergate investigators continued their prosecution of the individuals involved in the scandal.

Ehrlichman was eventually convicted of perjury and conspiracy to obstruct justice in the Watergate case, and of conspiracy in the Watergate-related Daniel Ellsberg case. He was sentenced to four to eight years in prison, but he served only 18 months before gaining his release.

After his release, Ehrlichman moved to New Mexico and became a novelist. A number of his works included thinly veiled attacks on Nixon and various high-ranking members of the ex-president's administration. "This is fiction with a hidden agenda: getting even," wrote one *Washington Post Book World* critic. As Ehrlichman tended his new career, he grew a beard and cultivated a reputation as a mellow and genial fellow—a marked departure from his stiff Watergate-era persona. In 1982 he published a memoir of the Watergate era called *Witness to Power: The Nixon Years.* The book was praised by some critics as entertaining and insightful, and panned by other reviewers as tedious and self-serving.

In 1991 Ehrlichman moved to Atlanta, where he worked as a business consultant. In 1996 dozens of pen-and-ink sketches that Ehrlichman had made during the Watergate era were featured in an Atlanta gallery exhibition. Ehrlichman died in Atlanta from diabetes on February 14, 1999.

Sources
Ehrlichman, John D. *Witness to Power: The Nixon Years.* New York: Simon and Schuster, 1982.

Weil, Martin. "Key Nixon Advisor John D. Ehrlichman Dies at 73." *Washington Post,* February 16, 1999.

Sam Ervin (1896-1985)
Conservative Democratic Senator from North Carolina

Chairman of the Senate Watergate Committee

Samuel James Ervin, Jr., was born in September 27, 1896, in Morganton, North Carolina, a community nestled in the foothills of the Blue Ridge Mountains. His parents were Samuel James Ervin, a successful self-educated lawyer, and Laura Theresa (Powe) Ervin. His father's fierce devotion to individual liberties and the U.S. Constitution made a lasting impression on young Sam during his childhood and adolescence, as did his emphasis on hard work and self-reliance.

Ervin decided to follow his father's career path. After earning a degree from the University of North Carolina in 1917, his education was interrupted by World War I. Ervin served in the army, where he became a decorated war hero. After returning home, he earned a law degree from Harvard Law School in 1922. He then returned to Morganton and became junior partner in the family law practice. In 1924 he married Margaret Bruce Bell, with whom he eventually had three children.

Ervin devoted most of his energies to the law, which he always described as his "first love." But he also served three terms in the North Carolina state assembly during the 1930s. In 1938 he accepted an appointment to become a state judge. In 1945 he returned to private practice, but his time in Morganton was brief. In 1946 he joined the U.S. House of Representatives after the elected representative—his brother, Joseph Ervin—died in office.

Joins the U.S. Senate

In 1948 Ervin was appointed to the North Carolina Supreme Court. Six years later, the governor of North Carolina asked Ervin to fill another political office that had been left vacant by the death of a sitting official—U.S. Senator Clyde Hoey. Ervin agreed to the request, and he spent the next two decades serving the people of North Carolina as one of their two representatives in the U.S. Senate.

During the 1950s and 1960s, Ervin became one of North Carolina's most popular politicians. At first glance, his voting record during this time appears inconsistent. For example, he fiercely opposed new federal civil rights legislation. But he also championed a variety of civil liberties measures, including an "Indian Bill of Rights" for Native Americans. He consistently supported American military involvement in Vietnam, but he denounced efforts to harass antiwar activists for their beliefs. He railed against court rulings that freed criminal suspects on "technicalities," yet he opposed many efforts to expand police powers against American citizens. In 1970, for instance, Ervin described one of Nixon's anticrime bills as "a garbage pail of the most repressive, near-sighted, intolerant, unfair and vindictive legislation that the Senate has ever been presented."

Ervin also expressed anger and disappointment with the quality of journalism in the United States at times. Yet he stood as one of the Senate's leading defenders of the First Amendment, the cornerstone of the nation's tradition of a free and independent press.

In actuality, Ervin's positions on these issues reflected his unchanging devotion to certain basic principles. When examining any issue, he always based his stand on his reading of the U.S. Constitution and on his own deep convictions about the importance of individual freedom and states' rights. When looked at in this light, Ervin's voting record in the Senate was a model of consistency.

Tapped to Head Watergate Investigation

By 1973, when the U.S. Senate decided to conduct a formal investigation into the Watergate scandal, Ervin was one of the best-liked and most respected lawmakers in the Senate. This quality, combined with his legal background and his disinterest in running for the presidency, made Ervin the ideal candidate to lead the Watergate committee—officially known as the Select Committee on Presidential Campaign Activities.

Ervin formally opened the hearings by the committee—which quickly came to be known as the Watergate Committee or the Ervin Committee—on May 17, 1973. In his opening remarks, Ervin stated that the committee's specific responsibility was to look into charges that the Committee for the Re-election of the President had engaged in criminal activity to help President Richard Nixon win a second term. But the North Carolina senator added that in a larger sense, the responsibility of committee members was to "probe into assertions that [America's political] system had been subverted."

Over the next seven weeks, Ervin presided over testimony that strongly suggested that Nixon and his inner circle of White House aides had engaged in all sorts of illegal activities. As the nationally televised hearings progressed, many Americans became extremely angry and disheartened by what they saw. But they also took comfort in Ervin's clear desire to get to the bottom of the Watergate mess. In fact, the folksy but determined Ervin became a celebrity of sorts. "In a few short weeks, this self-proclaimed country lawyer became a national symbol of decency and fairness in politics, the embodiment for many of wisdom, a genuine American folk hero," wrote Ervin biographer Paul Clancy in *Just a Country Lawyer*.

During the course of its investigation, the Ervin Committee discovered that Nixon taped all of his conversations in the Oval Office and certain other areas of the White House. Certain that these tapes would reveal whether Nixon was being truthful to the American people, the Ervin Committee and the Watergate Special Prosecution Force got subpoenas for the tapes. Nixon refused to turn the tapes over for months, citing "executive privilege." Ervin ridiculed Nixon's position as a cynical and transparent effort to avoid punishment.

Nixon eventually was forced to turn over the tapes, and on August 9, 1974, he resigned. In September 1974 President Gerald R. Ford pardoned his predecessor. Ervin publicly criticized the decision to pardon Nixon as "incompatible with good government…. [Pardons] are for the guilty—not for those who profess their innocence."

Uses Retirement Years to Write Autobiography

Ervin retired from the Senate in late 1974. His retirement prompted an outpouring of gratitude and appreciation for his years of service from lawmakers, newspapers, and North Carolinians alike. Ervin then returned to Morganton, where he led a happy and fulfilling existence.

Americans' memories of Ervin's steady hand during the Watergate hearings made him a popular draw on the lecture circuit, so he gave many speeches on college campuses and in front of professional and business groups. Many of his speeches and lectures focused on his lifelong passion for the U.S. Constitution.

Ervin also wrote three books during his retirement. The first of these books, *The Whole Truth: The Watergate Conspiracy*, was published in 1981 partly as a response to Nixon's 1978 memoirs. Angered by many of the assertions in Nixon's book, Ervin's book gave his own plainspoken perspective on the Watergate scandal—including Nixon's culpability in the affair.

In 1983 Ervin published *Humor of a Country Lawyer*, a collection of stories collected during his wide-ranging career. One year later, he published an autobiography called *Preserving the Constitution*. The book focused on the many ways the author defended the constitution as an attorney, judge, and politician. It was warmly praised by critics such as *Washington Post Book World*, which described it as "an interesting book about an interesting man's extraordinary life." Ervin died from respiratory and kidney failure on April 23, 1985, in Winston-Salem, North Carolina.

Sources

Clancy, Paul R. *Just a Country Lawyer: A Biography of Senator Sam Ervin.* Bloomington: Indiana University Press, 1974.

Dabney, Dick. *A Good Man: The Life of Sam J. Ervin.* New York: Houghton Press, 1976.

Ervin, Sam. *Preserving the Constitution: The Autobiography of Senator Sam J. Ervin, Jr.* Charlottesville, VA: Michie Co., 1984.

Ervin, Sam. *The Whole Truth: The Watergate Conspiracy.* New York: Random House, 1981.

H. R. Haldeman (1926-1993)
Chief of Staff to President Nixon

Leading Figure in the Watergate Cover-Up

Harry Robins Haldeman was born on October 27, 1926, in Los Angeles, California. Raised in Beverly Hills, he adopted the nickname "Bob" at an early age to distinguish himself from his father, Harry Francis Haldeman. After graduating from high school, Haldeman enrolled at the University of Redlands. He later moved on to the University of Southern California (USC) and the University of California at Los Angeles (UCLA), where he earned a bachelor's degree in 1948.

A member of the Naval Reserve during World War II, Haldeman developed strong conservative political views by the late 1940s. In 1949 he married Joanne Horton and took a job in New York with the J. Walter Thompson advertising agency.

In 1956 Haldeman took his first significant steps into national politics, when he joined the successful Republican effort to re-elect President Dwight Eisenhower and Vice-President Richard Nixon. In 1959 he took a sabbatical from J. Walter Thompson, where he had risen to an executive position, in order to support Nixon's unsuccessful campaign for the presidency. As the presidential contest progressed, Haldeman established a close personal and professional relationship with Nixon.

In 1961 Haldeman agreed to spearhead Nixon's campaign to win California's governorship. Decisively beaten in the governor's race, Nixon announced his intention to retire from politics. But in 1968 he made a dramatic political comeback. Encouraged by Haldeman and other political allies, Nixon seized the Republican presidential nomination and won the White House over Democratic nominee Hubert Humphrey. Haldeman's effective campaign management—and in particular his success at reshaping public perceptions of the candidate—were cited as key factors in Nixon's narrow victory.

Gatekeeper at the White House

Nixon promptly named Haldeman as his chief of staff, a position he relished. Haldeman established himself as an all-powerful "gatekeeper" to the Oval Office, severely restricting access to the president. As Nixon's chief aide, he also exerted considerable influence over the president's policy and political decisions. Haldeman's intimidating and condescending style, however, has been frequently cited as a key factor in the strained relations that developed between the Nixon administration and the national media.

Haldeman also helped engineer Nixon's lopsided re-election over Democratic candidate George McGovern in November 1972. But illegal activities undertaken on behalf of the Nixon re-election campaign—specifically the break-in at the Watergate office and apartment complex in Washington, D.C.—came back to haunt the president and his inner circle.

When Nixon, Haldeman, and other top aides learned of the break-in, they immediately conspired to cover-up the burglars' links to the Nixon White House and his re-election campaign. One of the most notable meetings on the subject took place between Haldeman and the president on June 23, 1972. Two years later, Nixon was forced to surrender a tape recording of this long conversation, described by investigators as the "smoking gun" that proved Nixon's deep involvement in the cover-up scheme.

As the Watergate scandal grew, Haldeman remained deeply committed to keeping both himself and Nixon out of trouble. But links between the scandal and the chief of staff became so apparent that Nixon finally asked Haldeman to submit his resignation. Haldeman objected to the move but obeyed. Nixon announced the departure of Haldeman and a number of other White House figures implicated in the cover-up on April 30, 1973.

Testifies Before the Watergate Committee

Even after his ouster, Haldeman strongly defended the president. On July 30, 1973, he began his nationally televised testimony before the Senate Watergate Committee with a firm declaration that "President Nixon had no knowledge of or involvement in either the Watergate affair itself or the subsequent efforts of a cover up.... I had no such knowledge or involvement."

In subsequent testimony, Haldeman praised Nixon as "one of America's greatest presidents." He also insisted that the president had fostered an atmosphere of "excitement, hard work, dedication, and accomplishment" in the White House. He repeatedly deflected blame away from the Oval Office and accused former White House Counsel John Dean of masterminding the cover-up without the knowledge of Nixon or himself.

Overall, the committee's efforts to use Haldeman's testimony to advance the investigation fizzled. Committee chief counsel Sam Dash recalled in his book *Chief Counsel* that "[Haldeman] appeared as an absent-minded witness who could not recall any details of practically anything that had happened during the relevant periods about which he was questioned."

But although Haldeman's appearance before the Senate Watergate Committee lacked the high drama of some other testimony, it did provide a glimpse into his perspective on the scandal. "Haldeman acknowledged that Watergate constituted a failure of some kind," summarized historian Stanley Kutler in *The Wars of Watergate*. "But in a note that he would sound for years afterward, he expressed puzzlement and bewilderment as to what that failure was, why it occurred, and who was responsible for it."

In 1975 Haldeman was convicted of perjury, obstruction of justice, and conspiracy to obstruct justice. He originally received a sentence of 30 months to eight years, but was released on appeal after serving 18 months. In 1976 he published a book on Watergate called *The Ends of Power,* which was roundly criticized as being vague and evasive on many subjects. The book did, however, acknowledge that both he and Nixon were involved in the cover-up from the beginning.

After his release from prison, Haldeman worked as a business consultant and in the real estate business. He also spent several years as a hotel executive and restaurant owner. He largely avoided the media spotlight in his later years, but friends described him as a mellow and amiable personality. He died of abdominal cancer on November 12, 1993, in Santa Barbara, California. The following year, his widow arranged for the publication of *The Haldeman Diaries*, a day-by-day record of his experiences in the Nixon administration during Watergate.

Sources
Dash, Samuel. *Chief Counsel: Inside the Ervin Committee—The Untold Story of Watergate.* New York: Random House, 1976.

Haldeman, H. R. *The Haldeman Diaries.* New York: Putnam, 1994.

Haldeman, H. R., with Joseph DiMona. *The Ends of Power.* New York: New York Times Books, 1978.

Kutler, Stanley. *The Wars of Watergate: The Last Crisis of Richard Nixon.* New York: Knopf, 1990.

Nixon, Richard M. *RN: The Memoirs of Richard Nixon.* New York: Grosset & Dunlap, 1978.

Leon Jaworski (1905-1982)
Second Watergate Special Prosecutor

Led the Investigation that Forced Nixon to Resign

Leonidas Jaworski was born on September 19, 1905, in Waco, Texas. He was the third child of a Polish father and Austrian mother who had immigrated to the United States to build a new life for themselves. Jaworski's father was an evangelical minister who spent several years as a circuit preacher, traveling to churches throughout the Waco area, before establishing his own church in town.

Jaworski finished high school at age 15 and began taking classes at Baylor University Law School one year later. He graduated in 1924, and a short time later became the youngest person in Texas history to pass the state bar. In 1926 he earned a master's degree in law from George Washington University in Washington, D.C.

Jaworski settled back in his home town of Waco, where he scratched out a lean existence "representing bootleggers and moonshiners [and] winning cases through his ability at cross-examining law officers and finding procedural errors," wrote assistant Watergate prosecutor James Doyle in *Not Above the Law*. "It was bootleggers or starvation for the new lawyer. The choice was easy."

A Reputation for Integrity

In 1929 Jaworski's name became known throughout Texas for his spirited—though ultimately unsuccessful—defense of a poor black tenant farmer named Jordan Scott who was accused of murdering a white couple. The case presented a nearly insurmountable challenge, as racial prejudice was so strong in the region that lynchings remained commonplace. Nonetheless, Jaworski defended his client with such righteous vigor that he lost a number of friends by the end of the trial. His performance, however, also garnered notice from law offices throughout Texas. When the powerful Houston law firm Fulbright, Cooker, Freeman, and Bates offered him a position, he quickly accepted. Jaworski excelled in his new duties, and he became a partner in the firm at age 29.

Jaworski served in the army during World War II. After the war concluded, he stayed in Europe to assist at the Nuremberg War Crimes trials. During these months he spent most of his time supervising the prosecution of German officials connected to the notorious Dachau concentration camp.

In 1946 Jaworski returned to practicing law in Houston, where he was promoted to senior partner. During the 1950s and 1960s he further enhanced his reputation as a sharp and shrewd attorney and businessman. He cultivated rewarding relationships with many of Texas's leading politicians and business executives. But he also adopted a progressive mindset toward various social issues, undeterred by opposition from his more conservative peers. For example, he was instrumental in making his law firm the first Houston-area firm to hire Jews, blacks, and women as attorneys.

From 1962 to 1965 Jaworski spent some time working in the Justice Department under Attorney General Robert F. Kennedy. In addition, he served on a number of presidential commissions during the administration of Lyndon B. Johnson. In July 1971 he began a 12-month stint as the president of the American Bar Association.

Succeeded Cox as Watergate Prosecutor

In 1973 the Watergate scandal became front-page news across the United States. Jaworski followed events closely, and like most other Americans, he was disturbed by Nixon's decision to fire Watergate Special Prosecutor Archibald Cox on October 20, 1973. Several days later, Jaworski was approached about succeeding Cox as special prosecutor. Jaworski accepted, and Nixon formally announced the appointment on November 1.

Nixon hoped that Jaworski would conduct his Watergate investigation in a less relentless fashion than had Cox. "[Nixon Chief of Staff Alexander] Haig liked Jaworski and was impressed by him," recalled Nixon in his memoirs. "He told me that Jaworski would be a tough prosecutor but not a partisan who was simply out to get me." As it turned out, however, Jaworski pursued the investigation with the same zeal as his predecessor. Moreover, Jaworski's political and professional reputation made it impossible for Nixon to paint him as someone with a political vendetta.

Jaworski was initially viewed with some suspicion by Cox's staff. Still angry about Cox's dismissal, they openly questioned whether the new special prosecutor would take it easy on Nixon. But Jaworski retained the existing staff rather than bringing in new investigators, and he repeatedly stood his ground with the White House in negotiations over the infamous Watergate tapes. These actions reassured staffers that he was pursuing the case with the same zeal as their former boss—and restored public confidence in the independence of his office.

Yet Jaworski's relations with Nixon never deteriorated to the poisonous level of the Cox-Nixon battles. "Partly from his southern manner and partly from his horse-trading instincts, Leon Jaworski is very good at being agreeable without agreeing to anything," explained Doyle. "Haig had often told White House aides that Jaworski was completely sympathetic to the president's problems but was unable to control the staff he inherited from Cox."

When Nixon resigned from office in August 1974, Jaworski directed his staff to prepare criminal charges against the former president. But when President Gerald R. Ford pardoned Nixon for his Watergate crimes in September 1974, Jaworski called a halt to these efforts. He also refused to criticize Ford for his decision to pardon his predecessor.

On October 25, 1974, Jaworski left Washington, D.C., and returned to Houston and resumed his law practice. He was succeeded as Watergate special prosecutor by Henry S. Ruth, Jr., who secured the convictions of several top White House aides for Watergate transgressions. Jaworski died on December 9, 1982, in Wimberley, Texas.

Sources

Jaworski, Leon. *The Right and the Power: The Prosecution of Watergate.* New York: Reader's Digest Press, 1976.

Jaworski, Leon, and Mickey Herskowitz. *Confession and Avoidance: A Memoir.* Garden City, NY: Anchor Press/Doubleday, 1979.

Doyle, James. *Not Above the Law: The Battles of Watergate Prosecutors Cox and Jaworski.* New York: Morrow, 1977.

John Mitchell (1913-1988)
Attorney General in Nixon Administration, 1969-1972

Director of Nixon's Re-Election Campaign

John Newton Mitchell was born September 15, 1913, in Detroit, Michigan. He was the only child of Joseph Charles Mitchell, a businessman, and Margaret Agnes McMahon. After graduating from high school in 1931, he enrolled at Fordham University. Once he earned his bachelor's degree in 1935, he decided to pursue a law degree at Fordham Law School. During this time he married Elizabeth Katherine Shine, with whom he had two children; they divorced in December 1957. On December 30, 1957, Mitchell married Martha Beall Jennings, with whom he had one child.

After earning his law degree from Fordham in 1938, Mitchell joined a Manhattan law firm, where he became an expert on municipal bonds. He was made a partner in the firm in 1942. His law career was interrupted by America's entrance into World War II. During the conflict Mitchell served in the Pacific Theatre as a commander of torpedo boat squadrons.

When the war concluded, Mitchell returned to his law practice at Caldwell, Trimble, and Mitchell. During the late 1940s and 1950s he became known for his financial acumen and his ability to handle bond financing for an array of public works construction, including universities, hospitals, and housing developments.

Mitchell Becomes Part of Nixon's Inner Circle

In 1967 Mitchell's law firm merged with a California firm that had former Vice President Richard Nixon as one of its partners. Within months of the creation of the firm—known as Nixon, Mudge, Rose, Guthrie, Alexander, and Mitchell—Nixon and Mitchell had developed a friendship based on mutual admiration.

When Nixon decided to seek the Republican nomination for the 1968 presidential election, he selected Mitchell as his chief campaign manager and advisor. By all accounts, Mitchell did a terrific job of emphasizing Nixon's strengths as a politician and campaigner—and of minimizing his vulnerabilities. He also helped Nixon develop his campaign's "law and order" themes. In addition, he was an enthusiastic proponent of the Republican Party's "Southern strategy," which aimed to attract socially conservative working-class white Southerners away from their traditional support for the Democratic Party.

When Nixon narrowly won election to the White House, he named Mitchell as his administration's attorney general, the highest law enforcement position in the land. Mitchell subsequently used his powers to redirect the nation's law enforcement resources toward "radicals," who were seen as threats to the country's social fabric and to the Nixon administration. Before long, political opponents of the White House also came to be seen as "enemy forces" by Mitchell and top White House advisors with whom the attorney general regularly consulted.

"The Nixon administration made government into an instrument of revenge and retaliation," wrote historian Michael Genovese. In fact, numerous official policies were eventually struck down by the courts as unconstitutional, and many of the secret activities approved by Mitchell and his aides were blatantly illegal. The most fateful of these secret schemes was a January 1972 meeting between Mitchell and several aides with the White House and the Committee to Re-Elect the President (CREEP). During the course of this meeting, Mitchell signed off on a program of illegal activities—including burglary and electronic surveillance—that promised to give CREEP a competitive advantage over its political adversaries. Reassured that he was following the wishes of the Nixon White House, CREEP Chief Counsel G. Gordon Liddy devised a plan to break in to Democratic National Committee headquarters in the Watergate office and apartment complex in Washington, D.C.

Director of Nixon Re-Election Campaign

On March 1, 1972, Mitchell left his position as attorney general in order to become director of CREEP. On June 18, he learned that several men with connections to the White House and the president's re-election campaign had been arrested in connection with a burglary at the Watergate complex. Nixon

109

and his inner circle of advisors hurriedly constructed a cover-up plan to conceal the administration's links to the burglars.

On July 1, 1972, Mitchell resigned his post with Nixon's re-election campaign, a decision that clearly relieved the president. Nixon and top White House advisors like H. R. Haldeman and John Ehrlichman spent much of the next number of months angling to make Mitchell the primary scapegoat for the blossoming scandal. They sought at every turn to characterize the Watergate affair as a rogue CREEP operation of which they had no knowledge. Yet Mitchell never turned on his former boss. In fact, he repeatedly praised Nixon's performance as president during his tense and testy appearance before the Senate Watergate Committee. The most notable other aspect of Mitchell's testimony was his revealing mention of "White House horrors"—a reference to the abuses of power that were rampant in the Nixon administration.

The whole situation infuriated Martha Mitchell, who knew about some aspects of the cover-up. Discouraged by her husband's refusal to testify against Nixon and outraged by the administration's efforts to make him the fall guy, she publicly called for the president's resignation. At one point she also told the *New York Times* that she feared for her husband's safety, and implied that the administration might try to frame him for Watergate crimes. The strain of the Watergate scandal eventually proved too much for their marriage. John and Martha Mitchell separated in 1973, and she died of bone cancer in May 1976.

In May 1973 Mitchell and former Nixon Commerce Secretary Maurice Stans were charged with interfering with a government investigation of financier Robert Vesco in return for a $200,000 contribution to Nixon's re-election effort. Eleven months later, however, both Mitchell and Stans were acquitted.

In the case of Watergate, Mitchell was not as fortunate. In March 1974 he was indicted on various charges associated with the scandal. He pleaded not guilty, but on New Year's Day 1975 he was found guilty of conspiracy, obstruction of justice, and perjury. He received a sentence of 30 months to eight years in prison. Mitchell thus became the first attorney general in U.S. history to serve time in prison.

Mitchell spent 19 months in prison in Alabama before gaining his release in January 1979. He subsequently worked as a business and public policy consultant in Washington, D.C. He died of a heart attack on November 9, 1988.

Sources

Genovese, Michael A. *The Watergate Crisis.* Westport, CT: Greenwood Press, 1999.

Higgins, George V. The *Friends of Richard Nixon.* Boston: Little, Brown, 1975.

McLendon, Wizola. Martha: *The Life of Martha Mitchell.* New York: Random House, 1979.

Nixon, Richard M. *RN: The Memoirs of Richard Nixon.* New York: Grosset & Dunlap, 1978.

Sussman, Barry. *The Great Coverup: Nixon and the Scandal of Watergate.* 3d ed. Arlington, VA: Seven Locks Press, 1992.

Richard M. Nixon (1913-1994)
37th President of the United States

Resigned the Presidency as a Result of Watergate

Richard Milhous Nixon was born on January 9, 1913, in the farming community of Yorba Linda, California. His parents were Frank and Hannah Milhous Nixon, and he was the second-oldest child in a family of five boys. The Nixon family struggled to maintain a middle-class economic standing throughout young Richard's childhood and adolescence. Frank Nixon, who labored as a carpenter, lemon grower, grocer, and gas station manager, has been characterized as a hard-working but angry man who harbored grievances against Eastern "elitists" and others of higher social status. Hannah Nixon, meanwhile, was a strong-willed, demanding mother from a prominent Quaker family. Nixon's memoirs portray her as the glue that kept the family together despite bouts of economic difficulty and the serious health troubles of Harold Nixon, Richard's older brother.

Nixon graduated from Whittier High School in 1930 and subsequently enrolled at Whittier College. He made a significant mark at Whittier, winning election as student-body president and emerging as one of the school's best debaters. After earning a bachelor's degree in 1934, he gained admission into the newly established law school at Duke University. He graduated in 1937, but his attempts to find employment with a New York law firm or the Federal Bureau of Investigation (FBI) were unsuccessful.

Nixon decided to return to Whittier, where he joined a modest law office. He married Thelma Catherine "Pat" Ryan on June 21, 1940. They eventually had two daughters, Patricia and Julie. In 1942 Nixon enlisted in the U.S. Navy and served as a quartermaster in the South Pacific. By his own account, Nixon won large amounts of money playing poker during his time in the military. He later said that he used these winnings to help fund his first run for political office in 1946.

112

Launches Career in Politics

When Nixon returned to Whittier after the war, Republican Party officials selected him to run against popular Democratic incumbent Jerry Voorhis for his 12th district seat in the U.S. House of Representatives. The race brought Nixon's political ambitions to life, and he quickly showed an instinct for ruthless political maneuvering. He launched a campaign in which he slandered his opponent as a pawn of Communist forces. The strategy reflected the "Cold War" hysteria that was gripping many American communities at the time, and Nixon rode this anti-Communist fervor to a comfortable victory. But the triumph came at a cost, for as Stanley Kutler pointed out in *The Wars of Watergate*, "nothing shaped the basic historical perception of Richard Nixon more than his first campaign for public office."

Nixon entered Congress in January 1947 and was assigned seats on both the House Labor Committee and the House Un-American Activities Committee (HUAC). The former was considered the more prestigious assignment, but it was Nixon's tenure with HUAC that lifted him to national prominence. Keenly aware of the American public's growing fear that the nation was riddled with Communist agents and sympathizers, he successfully cast himself as a leading Republican spokesman on the issue.

Nixon became even more prominent in mid-1948, when he staked his political career on a HUAC investigation into charges that State Department official Alger Hiss was a Communist agent. Hiss maintained his innocence during and after the Nixon-led investigation, but he was eventually found guilty of two counts of perjury. Years later, Nixon pointed to the still-controversial Alger Hiss case as one of the "six crises" that fundamentally shaped his political views.

In 1950 Nixon decided to run for an open California seat in the U.S. Senate. After clinching the Republican nomination, he turned his sights on his Democratic opponent, a liberal congresswoman named Helen Gahagan Douglas. The clash between the Nixon and Douglas camps was by all accounts one of the ugliest and most hateful political fights in California state history. Ultimately, however, the Douglas forces had no answer for Nixon's masterful use of negative campaign tactics. Branded by the Nixon campaign as a "pink lady" for her alleged sympathy for Communism, Douglas lost the election by more than 600,000 votes.

Nixon Becomes Vice President

The methods that Nixon employed to win a seat in the U.S. Senate troubled many observers. It also earned him the nickname "Tricky Dick," a name that dogged him for the rest of his political career. But his rapid political rise, his fearsome campaigning style, and his obvious ambition also made him a favorite of the Republican Party establishment.

In 1952 Nixon was selected by Republican presidential nominee Dwight Eisenhower, a noted World War II hero, to be his running mate. As the 1952 presidential campaign got underway, Nixon repeatedly assailed the policies and character of Democratic presidential nominee Adlai Stevenson. Democrats responded with withering attacks on Nixon, in part because of fears that criticisms of the popular Eisenhower would backfire with voters.

At one point, revelations that Nixon had used thousands of dollars from a secret political "slush fund" seemed to jeopardize his place on the ticket. Democrats pounced on the news to characterize Nixon as a man ethically unfit to serve as the country's vice president. But he defused the threat with a nationally televised address known as the "Checkers" speech, in which he declared that the only gift he had ever received was a cocker spaniel named Checkers. Democrats saw the speech as sappy, cynical, and manipulative, but it seemed to satisfy American voters.

In November 1952 the Eisenhower-Nixon ticket claimed the White House with 55 percent of the popular vote. As vice president, Nixon spent the bulk of his time on foreign policy issues. He also engaged in frequent and highly public sparring with Democrat leaders on administration positions. Nixon's willingness to trade verbal blows with political opponents undoubtedly diverted some partisan fire toward him and away from the president. But Eisenhower and Nixon never developed a comfortable working relationship. Eisenhower harbored doubts about Nixon's character, and his concerns about the Vice President's ethics were fed by close aides who felt similarly. According to Kutler, Eisenhower's secretary summed up the feelings of many of Eisenhower's inner circle when she commented that "the Vice President sometimes seems like a man who is acting like a nice man rather than being one."

By the beginning of the 1956 presidential campaign, Nixon had become such a controversial figure in American politics that some Republicans openly urged Eisenhower to choose a new running mate. But Nixon and his advisors quelled the "dump Nixon" movement, enabling him to keep his spot on the ticket.

Eisenhower marched to re-election in the November 1956 contest, and Nixon settled in for another term. His time was primarily taken up with foreign affairs and verbal firefights with the Democrats over various policy issues. But Eisenhower was also troubled by poor health at various times from 1955 through the end of his second term, and Nixon reportedly handled his increased responsibilities during these episodes in a calm and steady manner.

Nixon vs. Kennedy

When Eisenhower completed his second term, Nixon had a clear path to his party's presidential nomination. Endorsed by the still-popular Eisenhower, Nixon easily won the Republican Party's nomination for President. He would run against Democratic nominee John F. Kennedy, a U.S. senator from Massachusetts. The contest was close throughout, as Nixon fought to keep the upper hand over the articulate Kennedy and a Democratic Party that had made major gains in the 1958 Congressional elections. "Of the five presidential campaigns in which I was a direct participant," Nixon recalled in *RN: The Memoirs of Richard Nixon,* "none affected me more personally…. It was a campaign of unusual intensity."

The campaign also featured four presidential debates, including the first nationally televised debate ever held. In this first debate, Nixon held his own in the debate itself. But he appeared poorly groomed and haggard in comparison to Kennedy, who appeared poised and well-rested. The contrast made an impression in the mind of the American voting public, and Nixon's solid performances in the three later debates failed to repair the damage.

On election night, Kennedy and running mate Lyndon B. Johnson narrowly defeated Nixon and his vice-presidential nominee, Henry Cabot Lodge. The loss devastated Nixon, in part—according to some biographers—because the election results seemed to confirm his deepest personal insecurities and self-doubts. Kennedy was a glamorous, handsome, self-assured politician from a wealthy and powerful Eastern family; he thus possessed all the characteristics that Nixon had always envied in others.

Nixon also blamed the media for his defeat. He claimed that they became so infatuated with Kennedy that they provided slanted coverage during the campaign's final months. He argued that they gave too much weight to stories that hurt his campaign and that they minimized questionable tactics and activities by Kennedy and his campaign. This belief colored Nixon's relations with the press for the remainder of his political career, including the last two years of his Watergate-wracked presidency.

Historians, however, say that Nixon bears some responsibility for his crushing loss to Kennedy. "[Nixon] polarized the public more than any other man of his era," wrote historian Stephen Ambrose in *Nixon: Ruin and Recovery.* "It is remarkable but probably true that in 1960, when he was only 47 years old, he was the most hated and feared man in America—and next to Eisenhower himself, the most admired and wanted. That the split was almost 50-50 was demonstrated in the election of 1960."

Nixon Claims the White House

In 1962 Nixon ran for governor of California. But his campaign seemed unfocused and disjointed from the outset, and he was defeated by incumbent Governor Edmund Gerald "Pat" Brown, Sr. Afterward, Nixon appeared to signal his intention to permanently retire from politics when he angrily told a crowd of reporters that "You won't have Nixon to kick around anymore, because, gentlemen, this is my last press conference."

Nixon settled in New York City, where he worked as a corporate lawyer. But he kept his hand in Republican politics, and in 1968 he made a dramatic political comeback. He built a formidable campaign machine that enabled him to beat Barry Goldwater and Nelson Rockefeller for the Republican presidential nomination. He then faced off against Democratic nominee Hubert Humphrey. Humphrey had been vice president to Lyndon B. Johnson, who had been so badly scarred by the Vietnam War that he decided not to seek re-election. The other major figure in the presidential race was Alabama Governor George Wallace, whose segregationist beliefs and pro-war stance had led him to launch an independent bid for the White House.

Nixon took full advantage of domestic turmoil over the Vietnam War and the social divisions wracking America. He linked Humphrey to unpopular policies at every turn while simultaneously displaying increased recognition of television's power as a campaign tool. In fact, Nixon and his aides used the media to unveil a "new Nixon" who was packaged as more warm and friendly than the old version. Finally, Nixon's political machine aggressively pursued a "Southern strategy." Under this plan, Nixon staked out stands on social issues that would appeal to the region's conservative white voters. This strategy attracted many traditional Democratic voters who were unhappy with that party's perceived drift to the left.

Nixon's "law and order" campaign proved just effective enough to win the Oval Office. He captured 43.4 percent of the popular vote, while Humphrey finished with 42.7 percent (Wallace attracted most of the remainder). Nixon won by a more comfortable margin in the Electoral College vote, earning 302 votes compared to 191 for Humphrey. At age 55, Nixon had finally seized the greatest political prize of all.

Nixon's First Term

Throughout the 1968 campaign, Nixon had implied that he had a secret plan to bring the Vietnam War to an end. After taking office, he used a policy of "Vietnamization"—turning the prosecution of the war over to South Vietnamese forces—that brought 100,000 American troops home by early 1970. This strategy was accepted by the American public and took a lot of steam out of the antiwar movement, which had staged large protests in opposition to the war in the late 1960s. But in April 1970 Nixon abruptly expanded the war by invading Cambodia, Vietnam's neighbor to the west. This escalation of the conflict triggered massive antiwar protests across America, including a protest at Kent State University that ended in tragedy when National Guardsmen shot and killed four unarmed students.

The Nixon administration continued to struggle with the war for the remainder of the president's first term. Domestic unrest over the war waned, however, as Nixon completed the withdrawal of American ground forces from Vietnam. The United States and North Vietnam finally signed a peace treaty in February 1973, paving the way for the withdrawal of most remaining American forces in the war-torn country. After the U.S. departure, North Vietnam carried on its war against South Vietnam, and in April 1975 the North Vietnamese completed their takeover of the country.

Nixon enjoyed far more success in other foreign policy areas. He opened diplomatic relations with Communist China, overcoming years of hostility and suspicion between the two nations. He also carried out successful negotiations with the Soviet Union on limiting the proliferation of nuclear weapons. Nixon's national security advisor, Henry Kissinger, played an important role in these and other foreign policy successes. By all accounts, the two men shared a deep conviction that political stability and U.S. interests trumped all other foreign policy considerations.

On the domestic front, Nixon adhered to the "law and order" philosophy he put forth on the campaign trail. He advocated tougher penalties for drug users and other lawbreakers. He also expressed particular hostility toward antiwar protestors and other "radicals." On economic matters, Nixon struggled to rein in inflation and other woes, in part because of big differences with the Democrat-controlled Congress. The president successfully reduced federal funding for some social programs, but adopted a moderate stance on other issues. For example, he found common ground with Democrats on some domestic policy initiatives, including significant environmental protection measures. These agreements eroded some of Nixon's support in the conservative wing of his own party.

Finally, Nixon's first term was notable for his adversarial relationship with the press. Convinced that the cooperative relationship that had long existed between government and media had been sundered by Vietnam, the Nixon White House routinely treated the news media with a skepticism that sometimes bordered on contempt. Perceiving most journalists to be potential threats to his political goals, the President kept them at arm's length except when he thought they could advance his policy goals. "It is true that of all the Presidents in this century, it is probably true, that I have less, as somebody has said, supporters in the press than any President," Nixon told reporters Rowland Evans and Robert Novak, who related this claim in their 1971 book *Nixon in the White House.*

Nixon Wins Re-Election

In 1972 Nixon and his vice president, Spiro Agnew, easily won re-election. They trounced the Democratic ticket of George McGovern and Sargent Shriver, winning 61 percent of the popular vote. But even though polls showed Nixon enjoying a comfortable lead throughout the campaign, he and his closest aides were so determined to win a crushing victory that they approved a wide range of illegal activities against the Democrats. These activities ranged from electronic surveillance to the dissemination of vicious rumors about political adversaries. One of the schemes that grew out of this war mentality was a plan to break into Democratic Party headquarters at the Watergate Hotel in Washington, D.C.

When the burglary was discovered in June 1972, Nixon and his inner circle of White House aides agreed to cover up the burglars' links to his administration and the Committee to Re-Elect the President. Over the next two years, Nixon engaged in an increasingly frantic effort to keep investigators at bay. As time passed, Nixon's Watergate strategy of deceit and stonewalling rested on his ability to withhold White House tape recordings. These recordings not only revealed the president's deep involvement in the cover-up, but also his administration's sordid history of criminal activity in other areas.

Nixon's cover-up scheme slowly disintegrated in the glare of multiple investigations. His reputation with the American people went into a startling tailspin that accelerated with each new revelation of unethical and illegal conduct. In the summer of 1974 Nixon's desperate attempts to use the concept of executive privilege to keep the White House tapes out of the hands of Watergate investigators ended in failure. On July 24, 1974, the U.S. Supreme Court issued a unanimous ruling that Nixon had to hand over the tapes.

As Nixon reluctantly prepared to release the tapes, the U.S. House of Representatives decisively moved to impeach the president and remove him from office. Rather than endure that humiliating scenario, Nixon resigned the presidency on August 9, 1974. That same day, vice president Gerald Ford took the presidential oath to become the nation's 38th president. Ford issued a full pardon to Nixon on September 8, 1974. Nearly two years later, on July 8, 1976, Nixon was disbarred by the New York State Supreme Court on charges of obstruction of justice connected with Watergate.

Life After the White House

In the first few years after Nixon's stunning fall from grace, he nursed his wounds in private. During the late 1970s, however, he slowly returned to public life. In 1977 he agreed to a series of televised interviews with David Frost, and the following year he published *RN: The Memoirs of Richard Nixon*. He addressed the Watergate scandal in these and other venues, but with the passage of time Nixon—and his supporters—minimized the importance of the scandal or ignored it altogether.

During the 1980s Nixon consciously tried to cast himself as an elder statesman of American politics. He wrote a series of books on various foreign policy subjects and occasionally weighed in on political controversies of the

House Republicans Express Relief Over Resignation

The House Judiciary Committee passed three articles of impeachment against President Nixon in July 1974. Ten Republicans on the 38-member committee initially voted against each of the impeachment articles. When Nixon resigned, however, these 10 representatives issued a statement expressing their deep "gratitude" that he "spared the nation additional agony." Their statement also included the following remarks:

> We know it has been said, and perhaps some will continue to say, that Richard Nixon was "hounded from office" by his political opponents and media critics. We feel constrained to point out, however, that it was Richard Nixon who impeded the FBI's investigation of the Watergate affair by wrongfully attempting to implicate the Central Intelligence Agency; it was Richard Nixon who created and preserved the evidence of that transgression and who, knowing that it had been subpoenaed by this Committee and the Special Prosecutor, concealed its terrible import, even from his own counsel, until he could do so no longer....

> The tragedy that finally engulfed Richard Nixon has many facets. One was the very self-inflicted nature of the harm. It is striking that such an able, experienced, and perceptive man, whose ability to grasp the global implications of events little noticed by others may well have been unsurpassed by any of his predecessors, should fail to comprehend the damage that accrued daily to himself, his Administration, and to the Nation, as day after day, month after month, he imprisoned the truth about his role in the Watergate cover-up so long and so tightly within the solitude of his Oval Office that it could not be unleashed without destroying his presidency.

day. In 1990 the Nixon Presidential Library and Birthplace opened its doors in Nixon's hometown of Yorba Linda.

Observers considered Nixon's actions during this period an obvious attempt to polish his historical reputation. Certainly, the ex-president's efforts to rehabilitate his image worked to some degree. He received sympathetic coverage in some of the country's leading newspapers and magazines, and some politicians and historians emphasized his strong record on foreign affairs. But many other Americans never forgave Nixon, declaring that he would never be able to escape the disgrace he had brought on himself.

Nixon's wife Pat died in 1993. Nixon died on April 22, 1994, in New York City after suffering a severe stroke. The April 27 funeral service for Nixon in Yorba Linda was attended by President Bill Clinton, all four living ex-presidents, and numerous heads of state from around the world.

Sources

Ambrose, Stephen E. *Nixon: The Education of a Politician, 1913-1962.* New York: Simon & Schuster, 1987.

Ambrose, Stephen E. *Nixon: The Triumph of a Politician, 1962-1972.* New York: Simon & Schuster, 1989.

Ambrose, Stephen E. *Nixon: Ruin and Recovery: 1973-1990.* New York: Simon & Schuster, 1991.

Evans, Rowland, Jr., and Robert Novak. *Nixon in the White House: The Frustration of Power.* New York: Random House, 1971.

Kutler, Stanley. *The Wars of Watergate: The Last Crisis of Richard Nixon.* New York: Norton, 1990.

Nixon, Richard. *In the Arena: A Memoir of Victory, Defeat and Renewal.* New York: Simon & Schuster, 1990.

Nixon, Richard. *RN: The Memoirs of Richard Nixon.* New York: Grosset & Dunlap, 1978.

Small, Melvin. *The Presidency of Richard Nixon.* Lawrence: University Press of Kansas, 1999.

Summers, Anthony. *The Arrogance of Power: The Secret World of Richard Nixon.* New York: Viking, 2000.

Sussman, Barry. *The Great Coverup: Nixon and the Scandal of Watergate.* 3d ed. Alexandria, VA: Seven Locks Press, 1992.

Wicker, Tom. *One of Us: Richard Nixon and the American Dream.* New York: Random House, 1991.

John J. Sirica (1904-1992)
Presiding Federal Court Judge on the Watergate Case

Issued the Subpoenas for Nixon's Watergate Tapes that Ultimately Compelled the President to Release the Tapes

John Joseph Sirica was born on March 19, 1904, in Waterbury, Connecticut. His parents were Ferdinand "Fred" Sirica, an Italian immigrant, and Rose (Zinno) Sirica, whose parents had emigrated from Italy. They had one other son, Andrew. Fred Sirica supported his family as a barber, but family finances and struggles with tuberculosis prompted him to seek work in the American South and West.

This nomadic existence came to an end for John when he was 14 years old. The Sirica family settled in Washington, D.C., and John enrolled in George Washington Law School at age 17. Sirica's limited schooling left him badly unprepared for the school's coursework, and he dropped out within a matter of weeks. He then supported himself as a boxer and boxing instructor (the famous boxer Jack Dempsey, his lifelong friend, served as his best man when Sirica wed in 1952). A few years later, he returned to school, earning a law degree from Georgetown University Law School in 1926.

Over the next three decades, Sirica spent most of his time in private practice, but he also served a four-year stint (1930-1934) as a prosecutor on the staff of the U.S. Attorney General. He also became an active participant in Republican Party causes, working on five successive presidential campaigns beginning in 1936. In 1952 he married Lucile M. Camalier, with whom he raised two daughters and one son.

In 1957 Republican President Dwight D. Eisenhower appointed Sirica to the U.S. District Court for the District of Columbia. This appointment was partly a nod to his success as a lawyer, but was also attributed to his steady support for Republican political causes. After ascending to the federal bench, Sirica garnered a reputation as a blunt, hardworking judge with a penchant for handing out the longest prison sentences permissible by law. He acquired the nickname "Maximum John" as a result.

During his years on the bench, Sirica's decisions were overturned on appeal with greater frequency than those of other judges. This trend was traced to the judge's impatience with complex legal maneuvering and his maverick temperament. Nonetheless, due to longstanding rules of seniority, Sirica became chief judge of the U.S. District Court on April 2, 1971. The authority of this position enabled Sirica to claim the Watergate case for himself rather than assign it to another judge.

Pursuing the Truth in the Watergate Affair

Prior to the Watergate affair, Sirica had presided over a wide array of complex and high-profile civil and criminal cases. But unlike any of these cases, the Watergate burglary transformed Judge Sirica into a nationally known figure. In fact, his actions as judge in the Watergate case led *Time* magazine to name Sirica its 1973 Man of the Year. By "stubbornly and doggedly pursuing the truth in his courtroom regardless of its political implications," wrote *Time*, "[Sirica] forced Watergate into the light of investigative day."

Sirica began presiding over the trials of the Watergate burglars—seven men who had been arrested in connection with the burglary of Democratic Party headquarters in Washington, D.C.—on January 10, 1973. As the legal proceedings unfolded, Sirica quickly came to the conclusion that the defendants were lying about various aspects of the break-in. Sirica did not conceal his skepticism about their testimony. In fact, the judge used his authority to aggressively question the defendants about the burglary. He warned them that if anyone else was involved in the break-in, "I want to know it and the grand jury wants to know it." He also openly scoffed at some of their claims—such as their insistence that they had no idea where they got the money to carry out the burglary operation.

At the end of January, when all seven burglars either made guilty pleas or were convicted, Sirica applied pressure once again. He handed down severe "provisional" sentences that would only be reduced if the burglars cooperated with investigators. "I am still not satisfied that all of the pertinent facts have been produced before an American jury," he explained.

Some legal authorities questioned these sentences, which they described as extortion. Sirica's energetic questioning of the Watergate defendants also

drew some criticism from scholars who felt that he behaved more like a prosecutor than a judge. Sirica, however, dismissed these complaints. "I don't
think [judges] should sit up here like nincompoops," he said in *To Set the
Record Straight.* "The function of a trial court is to search for the truth."

In March 1973, one of the Watergate burglars, James McCord, approached
Sirica with an offer to provide more information in exchange for a reduced sentence. Historians believe that McCord might never have come forward had it
not been for the judge's tough stance. Over the next several months, the information provided by McCord and others on trial before Sirica proved vital in
revealing White House involvement in the Watergate break-in and cover-up.

Battling with President Nixon

As the Watergate investigation deepened, Sirica repeatedly crossed
swords with President Richard Nixon and the Nixon White House. Once the
existence of a White House tape recording system became known, Sirica consistently supported the efforts of the Senate Watergate Committee and Special
Prosecutors Archibald Cox and Leon Jaworski to gain access to those tapes.
In a thoughtful legal opinion, Sirica rejected Nixon's claim that the tapes were
protected by "executive privilege." "In all candor," Sirica summarized, "the
court fails to perceive any reason for suspending the power of courts to get
evidence and rule on questions of privilege in criminal matters simply
because it is the President of the United States who holds the evidence."

In December the White House grudgingly turned over to Sirica seven
subpoenaed tapes. Sirica carefully listened to the tapes in private. He eventually upheld claims of executive privilege or irrelevance on all or parts of three
tapes, then turned the remaining tapes over to Special Prosecutor Jaworski
and the grand jury. As Sirica listened to the tapes, he felt that they proved that
Nixon had been criminally involved in the Watergate cover-up. On January 9,
1974, Jaworski requested more White House tapes, but the Nixon White
House refused to honor Sirica's subpoena for the tapes.

Nixon continued to defy Sirica's subpoenas to release the Watergate tapes
until July 24, 1974, when the U.S. Supreme Court unanimously upheld Sirica's
order. When Nixon released the tapes a few days later, virtually all support for
the president vanished. He subsequently resigned from office on August 9, 1974.

After Nixon's resignation, Sirica presided over trials and sentencing of
various Watergate figures for the next three years. He stepped down as chief

judge of the court on his 70th birthday, in accordance with federal law. But he remained a full-time member of the bench until 1977, when he went into semi-retirement. In 1979 he published a memoir of his Watergate experiences called *To Set the Record Straight*, which included a spirited defense of his actions on the bench during the Watergate investigation. "I'm glad I did it," he stated. "If I had to do it over, I would do the same—and that's the end of that."

Sirica left the bench on October 1, 1986, and spent his retirement in Washington, D.C. He died of cardiac arrest at Georgetown University Hospital on August 14, 1992.

Sources

Jaworski, Leon. *The Right and the Power: The Prosecution of Watergate.* New York: Reader's Digest Press, 1976.

Martz, Larry. "John Sirica: A Man for His Season." *Newsweek,* August 24, 1992.

Sirica, John J. *To Set the Record Straight: The Break-In, the Tapes, the Conspirators, and the Pardon.* New York: Norton, 1979.

"TIME Person of the Year 1973: Judge John J. Sirica." *Time,* January 7, 1974.

PRIMARY SOURCES

John Dean Recalls the Early Days of the Watergate Cover-Up

In the days following the arrests of the Watergate burglars, the Nixon administration sprang into action. It labored mightily to minimize political damage from the arrests while simultaneously launching a massive cover-up of White House and CRP (Committee to Re-Elect the President) involvement in the burglary. White House Counsel John Dean, who became a principal figure in the cover-up, recalled these activities in this excerpt from his 1976 book, Blind Ambition.

Although the White House press machine conveyed a media image of Olympian disdain for so piddling a matter as the break-in, the truth could hardly have been more different. The scramble was on. People were worried about fingerprints. High officials were already playing dumb, even to each other, shoveling guilt out of their own offices. A pallor hung over conversations. Cover-up personalities were emerging. Colson adopted an enthusiastic know-nothing posture, unabashedly declaring his innocence, discovering exculpatory memos right and left in his characteristic whirlwind fashion. Haldeman exuded confidence, almost as distant from the mess as the President himself. Mitchell brooded and stewed quietly. Ehrlichman, sensing danger, moved in shrewdly behind a screen of fact-finding agents whom he maneuvered like chess pieces.

I had begun as a foil and go-between, but my extensive knowledge qualified me for a major role. From the beginning, I knew that the vulnerability of the Watergate affair spread broadly across the whole Administration. The lesser aides came to the counsel with confessions; the higher aides commenced to behave in a stealthy manner. I simply assumed, both from the facts I knew and from my knowledge of procedures in the White House, that the vulnerability went right into the President's office. Since I was still on the fringes of the inner circle, I did not know precisely how the President was reacting, but I worked from the premise that he needed protection....

The "stonewall" strategy functioned from the very first episodes of the cover-up. It was instinctive, from the very top of the Administration to the bottom. It was also ad hoc, developed in small reactions to the flurry of each day's events. There was not time to take stock of the whole case or to plan a careful defense in the meticulous fashion of trial lawyers. Instead, we found

---

ourselves trying to hold a line where we could. But the line could not be held at the Cubans and McCord; there was too much evidence implicating Hunt and Liddy. Almost immediately, we knew that the money used to pay for the break-in would be traced by the FBI to the Re-Election Committee. We conceded that and worked toward two goals: to explain the use of the money by claiming that Hunt and Liddy had diverted the funds on their own for illegitimate purposes, and to keep the FBI from tracing the money *backward* from the Re-Election Committee to its donors. Such a backward trace, we knew, could lead the FBI into what we called "other problems"—Campaign Act violations, unreported contributions, corporate contributions, secret contributions by nominal Democrats, and the like.

I began my role in the cover-up as a fact-finder and worked my way up to idea man, and finally to desk officer. At the outset, I sensed no personal danger in what I was doing. In fact, I took considerable satisfaction from knowing that I had no criminal liability, and I consistently sought to keep it that way…

Over time, however, Dean gradually emerged as one of the chief architects of the cover-up, and he engaged in various criminal activities to keep the cover-up intact. Dean frequently met with Nixon during this time, but their meetings did nothing to allay his growing fears that the cover-up would eventually be discovered.…

My sense of guilt was to deepen as I lost the few remaining rationalizations that I was acting as a low-level agent. Everyone betrayed a sense of guilt in meetings. I had managed for a while to evade it by contemplating the startling boost that Watergate had given me into the inner circles. My adult life had been calculated blindly and shrewdly, I had always thought. I was now reaching the pinnacle. I was not the source of authority for the cover-up, yet I became its linchpin. I was the only one with the knowledge and personal rapport to reconcile the pitched camps at the White House and the Re-Election Committee. I could feel my power growing in every meeting and each conversation as I went back and forth—resolving disputes between the warring factions and unwittingly linking and knitting them together in conspiracy…

Toward the end of January [1973], the outward signs were still good. The Watergate trial ended without major mishap, all seven defendants convicted. The President negotiated a settlement in Vietnam; his popularity in the polls rose to a high of 68 percent approval. These were bright spots that helped me hold together an optimistic front. Inside, I was dying…. The same mental predilections that had propelled me to the White House and into a leading role in the cover-up now made it impossible for my mind to ignore the grave weaknesses of our position....

The President still intimidated me, but I had lost a great deal of the romance. I also began to lose faith that the President could overcome the Watergate scandal by infinite power and wisdom. He seemed as enmeshed in it as the rest of us. I soon began to stop looking forward to these meetings; they no longer offered me confidence—about anything. The power fix, the high which I had pursued all my adult life, was wearing off. I was coming down.

Source: Dean, John. *Blind Ambition: The White House Years.* New York: Simon and Schuster, 1976.

The "Smoking Gun" Conversation Between Nixon and Haldeman

On June 23, 1972, President Richard Nixon and his chief of staff, H. R. Haldeman, held a meeting in the Oval Office to discuss the FBI's investigation of the Watergate break-in, including the agency's efforts to trace the source of the money found in the burglar's possession. During the course of this meeting, Nixon and Haldeman decide to smother the investigation because of concerns that it might reveal White House links to the burglars. They decide to pressure the leadership of the CIA to tell FBI investigators that the break-in was part of a failed intelligence operation, and that continuing the investigation could threaten national security.

The public release of this conversation, which was recorded on Nixon's secret White House taping system, came to be known as the "smoking gun" conversation, for it revealed that the president flatly lied to the American people when he asserted that he had not participated in the Watergate cover up. The following are excerpts from the tape transcript.

June 23, 1972, from 10:04 to 11:39 a.m.

Haldeman: ...Now, on the investigation, you know, the Democratic break-in thing, we're back to the—in the, the problem area because the FBI is not under control, because [acting FBI director L. Patrick] Gray doesn't exactly know how to control them, and they have, their investigation is now leading into some productive areas, because they've been able to trace the money, not through the money itself, but through the bank, you know, sources—the banker himself. And, and it goes in some directions we don't want it to go. Ah, also there have been some things, like an informant came in off the street to the FBI in Miami, who was a photographer or has a friend who is a photographer who developed some films through this guy, Barker [Bernard Barker, one of the Watergate burglars], and the films had pictures of Democratic National Committee letter head documents and things. So I guess, so it's things like that are gonna, that are filtering in. Mitchell came up with yesterday, and John Dean analyzed very carefully last night and concludes, concurs now with Mitchell's recommendation that the only way to solve this, and we're set up beautifully to do it, ah, in that and that ... the only network that paid any attention to it last night was NBC ... they did a massive story on the Cuban ...

Nixon: That's right.

Haldeman: ... thing.

132

Nixon: Right.

Haldeman: That the way to handle this now is for us to have [CIA Deputy Director Vernon] Walters call Pat Gray and just say, "Stay the hell out of this ... this is ah, business here we don't want you to go any further on it." That's not an unusual development ...

Nixon: Um huh.

Haldeman: ... and, uh, that would take care of it.

Nixon: What about Pat Gray, ah, you mean he doesn't want to?

Haldeman: Pat does want to. He doesn't know how to, and he doesn't have, he doesn't have any basis for doing it. Given this, he will then have the basis. He'll call [FBI Deputy Associate Director Mark] Felt in, and the two of them ... and Mark Felt wants to cooperate because ...

Nixon: Yeah.

Haldeman: ... he's ambitious ...

Nixon: Yeah.

Haldeman: ... ah, he'll call him in and say, "We've got the signal from across the river to, to put the hold on this." And that will fit rather well because the FBI agents who are working the case, at this point, feel that's what it is. This is CIA.

Nixon: But they've traced the money to 'em.

Haldeman: Well they have, they've traced to a name, but they haven't gotten to the guy yet.

Nixon: Would it be somebody here?

Haldeman: Ken Dahlberg.

Nixon: Who the hell is Ken Dahlberg?

Haldeman: He's ah, he gave $25,000 [to Nixon's re-election committee] in Minnesota and, ah, the check went directly in to this, to this guy Barker.

Nixon: Maybe he's a ... bum.... He didn't get this from the committee though, from [CREEP official Maurice] Stans.

Haldeman: Yeah. It is. It is. It's directly traceable and there's some more through some Texas people in—that went to the Mexican bank which they can also trace to the Mexican bank... they'll get their names today. And ...

Nixon: Well, I mean, ah, there's no way ... I'm just thinking if they don't cooperate [with investigators], what do they say? They, they were approached by the Cubans. That's what Dahlberg has to say, the Texans too. Is that the idea?

Haldeman: Well, if they will. But then we're relying on more and more people all the time. That's the problem. And ah, they'll stop if we could, if we take this other step.

Nixon: All right. Fine.

Haldeman: They say the only way to do that is from White House instructions. And it's got to be to [CIA Director Richard] Helms and, ah, what's his name? Walters.

Nixon: Walters.

Haldeman: And the proposal would be that Ehrlichman and I call them in ...

Nixon: All right, fine.

Haldeman: ... and say, ah ...

Nixon: How do you call him in, I mean you just, well, we protected Helms from one hell of a lot of things.

Haldeman: That's what Ehrlichman says.

Nixon: Of course, this is a, this is a [former CIA agent E. Howard] Hunt, you will—that will uncover a lot of things. You open that scab there's a hell of a lot of things and that we just feel that it would be very detrimental to have this thing go any further. This involves these Cubans, Hunt, and a lot of hanky-panky that we have nothing to do with ourselves. Well what the hell, did Mitchell know about this thing to any much of a degree?

Haldeman: I think so. I don't think he knew the details, but I think he knew.

Nixon: He didn't know how it was going to be handled though, with Dahlberg and the Texans and so forth? Well who was the asshole who did? (Unintelligible) Is it [CREEP legal counsel G. Gordon] Liddy? Is that the fellow? He must be a little nuts.

Haldeman: He is.

134

Nixon: I mean he just isn't well screwed on, is he? Isn't that the problem?

Haldeman: No, but he was under pressure, apparently, to get more information, and as he got more pressure, he pushed the people harder to move harder on ...

Nixon: Pressure from Mitchell?

Haldeman: Apparently.

Nixon: Oh, Mitchell, Mitchell was at the point that you made on this, that exactly what I need from you is on the—

Haldeman: Gemstone, yeah.

Nixon: All right, fine, I understand it all. We won't second-guess Mitchell and the rest. Thank God it wasn't [White House special counsel Charles] Colson.

Haldeman: The FBI interviewed Colson yesterday. They determined that would be a good thing to do.

Nixon: Um hum.

Haldeman: Ah, to have him take a ...

Nixon: Um hum.

Haldeman: An interrogation, which he did, and that, the FBI guys working the case had concluded that there were one or two possibilities, one, that this was a White House, they don't think that there is anything at the election committee, they think it was either a White House operation and they had some obscure reasons for it, non political ...

Nixon: Uh huh.

Haldeman: ... or it was a ...

Nixon: Cuban thing ...

Haldeman: Cubans and the CIA. And after their interrogation of, of ...

Nixon: Colson.

Haldeman: Colson, yesterday, they concluded it was not the White House, but are now convinced it is a CIA thing, so the CIA turn off would ...

Nixon: Well, not sure of their analysis, I'm not going to get that involved, I'm (unintelligible).

Haldeman: No, sir. We don't want you to.

Nixon: You call them in. Good. Good deal! Play it tough. That's the way they play it and that's the way we are going to play it.

Haldeman: O.K. We'll do it.

The conversation between Nixon and Haldeman then touches on a few other topics before returning to the subject of pressuring the CIA to put an end to the FBI investigation of the Watergate break-in. The two men agree that the CIA might cooperate if they tell agency officials that the investigation will re-open the so-called "Bay of Pigs" controversy—a reference to a 1961 CIA operation that failed miserably in its goal of overthrowing Cuba's Communist dictator Fidel Castro.

Nixon: When you get in these people when you ... get these people in, say: "Look, the problem is that this will open the whole, the whole Bay of Pigs thing, and the President just feels that" ah, without going into the details ... don't, don't lie to them to the extent to say there is no involvement, but just say this is sort of a comedy of errors, bizarre, without getting into it, "the President believes that it is going to open the whole Bay of Pigs thing up again. And, ah because these people are plugging for, for keeps and that they should call the FBI in and say that we wish for the country, don't go any further into this case," period!

Haldeman: O.K.

Nixon: That's the way to put it, do it straight (unintelligible).

Haldeman: Get more done for our cause by the opposition than by us at this point.

Nixon: You think so?

Haldeman: I think so, yeah.

Source: National Archives and Records Administration, http://www.archives.gov/nixon/
    tapes/transcripts/exhibit1.pdf

President Nixon Addresses the Nation about the Watergate Investigation

In late April 1973, President Richard M. Nixon secured the resignations of Chief of Staff H.R. Haldeman, Attorney General Richard Kleindienst, and Advisor John Ehrlichman. He also fired White House Counsel John Dean. On April 30, 1973, Nixon gave a nationally televised speech in which he explained his reasons for removing the men from their positions. This address marked Nixon's most detailed comments on the Watergate scandal up to that point. Following are excerpts from his April 30 address:

Good evening.

I want to talk to you tonight from my heart on a subject of deep concern to every American. In recent months, members of my Administration and officials of the Committee for the Re-Election of the President—including some of my closest friends and most trusted aides—have been charged with involvement in what has come to be known as the Watergate affair. These include charges of illegal activity during and preceding the 1972 Presidential election and charges that responsible officials participated in efforts to cover up that illegal activity.

The inevitable result of these charges has been to raise serious questions about the integrity of the White House itself. Tonight I wish to address those questions.

Last June 17, while I was in Florida trying to get a few days rest after my visit to Moscow, I first learned from news reports of the Watergate break-in. I was appalled at this senseless, illegal action, and I was shocked to learn that employees of the Re-Election Committee were apparently among those guilty. I immediately ordered an investigation by appropriate Government authorities. On September 15, as you will recall, indictments were brought against seven defendants in the case.

As the investigations went forward, I repeatedly asked those conducting the investigation whether there was any reason to believe that members of my Administration were in any way involved. I received repeated assurances that there were not. Because of these continuing reassurances, because I believed the reports I was getting, because I had faith in the persons from whom I was getting them, I discounted the stories in the press that appeared to implicate members of my Administration or other officials of the campaign committee.

Until March of this year, I remained convinced that the denials were true and that the charges of involvement by members of the White House staff were false. The comments I made during this period, and the comments made by my press secretary on my behalf, were based on the information provided to us at the time we made those comments. However, new information then came to me which persuaded me that there was a real possibility that some of these charges were true, and suggesting further that there had been an effort to conceal the facts both from the public, from you, and from me.

As a result, on March 21, I personally assumed the responsibility for coordinating intensive new inquiries into the matter, and I personally ordered those conducting the investigations to get all the facts and to report them directly to me, right here in this office.

I again ordered that all persons in the Government or at the Re-Election Committee should cooperate fully with the FBI, the prosecutors, and the grand jury. I also ordered that anyone who refused to cooperate in telling the truth would be asked to resign from government service. And, with ground rules adopted that would preserve the basic constitutional separation of powers between the Congress and the Presidency, I directed that members of the White House staff should appear and testify voluntarily under oath before the Senate committee which was investigating Watergate.

I was determined that we should get to the bottom of the matter, and that the truth should be fully brought out—no matter who was involved....

Today, in one of the most difficult decisions of my Presidency, I accepted the resignations of two of my closest associates in the White House—Bob Haldeman, John Ehrlichman—two of the finest public servants it has been my privilege to know.

I want to stress that in accepting these resignations, I mean to leave no implication whatever of personal wrongdoing on their part, and I leave no implication tonight of implication on the part of others who have been charged in this matter. But in matters as sensitive as guarding the integrity of our domestic process, it is essential not only that rigorous legal and ethical standards be observed but also that the public, you, have total confidence that they are both being observed and enforced by those in authority and particularly by the President of the United States. They agreed with me that this move was necessary in order to restore that confidence.

Because Attorney General Kleindienst—though a distinguished public servant, my personal friend for 20 years, with no personal involvement whatever in this matter—has been a close personal and professional associate of some of those who are involved in this case, he and I both felt that it was also necessary to name a new Attorney General.

The Counsel to the President, John Dean, has also resigned.

As the new Attorney General, I have today named Elliot Richardson, a man of unimpeachable integrity and rigorously high principle. I have directed him to do everything necessary to ensure that the Department of Justice has the confidence and the trust of every law-abiding person in this country.

I have given him absolute authority to make all decisions bearing upon the prosecution of the Watergate case and related matters. I have instructed him that if he should consider it appropriate, he has the authority to name a special supervising prosecutor for matters arising out of the case.

Whatever may appear to have been the case before, whatever improper activities may yet be discovered in connection with this whole sordid affair, I want the American people to know beyond the shadow of a doubt that during my term as President, justice will be pursued fairly, fully, and impartially, no matter who is involved. This office is a sacred trust and I am determined to be worthy of that trust....

Who, then, is to blame for what happened in this case?

For specific criminal actions by specific individuals, those who committed those actions must, of course, bear the liability and pay the penalty. For the fact that alleged improper activities took place within the White House or within my campaign organization, the easiest course would be for me to blame those to whom I delegated the responsibility to run the campaign. But that would be a cowardly thing to do.

I will not place the blame on subordinates—on people whose zeal exceeded their judgment and who may have done wrong in a cause they deeply believed to be right.

In any organization, the man at the top must bear the responsibility. That responsibility, therefore, belongs here, in this office. I accept it. And I pledge to you tonight, from this office, that I will do everything in my power to ensure that the guilty are brought to justice and that such abuses are purged from our political processes in the years to come, long after I have left this office.

Some people, quite properly appalled at the abuses that occurred, will say that Watergate demonstrates the bankruptcy of the American political system. I believe precisely the opposite is true. Watergate represented a series of illegal acts and bad judgments by a number of individuals. It was the system that has brought the facts to light and that will bring those guilty to justice—a system that in this case has included a determined grand jury, honest prosecutors, a courageous judge, John Sirica, and a vigorous free press.

It is essential now that we place our faith in that system—and especially in the judicial system. It is essential that we let the judicial process go forward, respecting those safeguards that are established to protect the innocent as well as to convict the guilty. It is essential that in reaction to the excesses of others, we not fall into excesses ourselves.

It is also essential that we not be so distracted by events such as this that we neglect the vital work before us, before this Nation, before America, at a time of critical importance to America and the world.

Since March, when I first learned that the Watergate affair might in fact be far more serious than I had been led to believe, it has claimed far too much of my time and my attention. Whatever may now transpire in the case, whatever the actions of the grand jury, whatever the outcome of any eventual trials, I must now turn my full attention—and I shall do so—once again to the larger duties of this office. I owe it to this great office that I hold, and I owe it to you—to my country....

I have been in public life for more than a quarter of a century. Like any other calling, politics has good people and bad people. And let me tell you, the great majority in politics—in the Congress, in the Federal Government, in the State government—are good people. I know that it can be very easy, under the intensive pressures of a campaign, for even well-intentioned people to fall into shady tactics—to rationalize this on the grounds that what is at stake is of such importance to the Nation that the end justifies the means. And both of our great parties have been guilty of such tactics in the past.

In recent years, however, the campaign excesses that have occurred on all sides have provided a sobering demonstration of how far this false doctrine can take us. The lesson is clear: America, in its political campaigns, must not again fall into the trap of letting the end, however great that end is, justify the means.

I urge the leaders of both political parties, I urge citizens, all of you, everywhere, to join in working toward a new set of standards, new rules and procedures to ensure that future elections will be as nearly free of such abuses as they possibly can be made. This is my goal. I ask you to join in making it America's goal.

When I was inaugurated for a second time this past January 20, I gave each member of my Cabinet and each member of my senior White House staff a special 4-year calendar, with each day marked to show the number of days remaining to the Administration. In the inscription on each calendar, I wrote these words: "The Presidential term which begins today consists of 1,461 days—no more, no less. Each can be a day of strengthening and renewal for America; each can add depth and dimension to the American experience. If we strive together, if we make the most of the challenge and the opportunity that these days offer us, they can stand out as great days for America, and great moments in the history of the world."

I looked at my own calendar this morning up at Camp David as I was working on this speech. It showed exactly 1,361 days remaining in my term. I want these to be the best days in America's history, because I love America. I deeply believe that America is the hope of the world. And I know that in the quality and wisdom of the leadership America gives lies the only hope for millions of people all over the world that they can live their lives in peace and freedom. We must be worthy of that hope, in every sense of the world. Tonight, I ask for your prayers to help me in everything that I do throughout the days of my Presidency to be worthy of their hopes and of yours.

God bless America and God bless each and every one of you.

Source: Richard Nixon Library and Birthplace Foundation, http://www.nixonfoundation. org/Research_Center/1973_pdf_files/1973_0134.pdf

Ervin and Baker React to President Nixon's Refusal to Release Watergate Tapes

On July 23, 1973, Richard Nixon sent a letter to Sam Ervin (Democrat-North Carolina), chairman of the Senate Watergate Committee, in response to the committee's request for tape recordings of presidential conversations. Nixon's letter informs Ervin that he will not turn over the tapes. Following is the full text of the letter.

D ear Mr. Chairman:

I have considered your request that I permit the Committee to have access to tapes of my private conversations with a number of my closest aides. I have concluded that the principles [of executive privilege] stated in my letter to you of July 6th preclude me from complying with that request, and I shall not do so. Indeed the special nature of tape recordings of private conversations is such that these principles apply with even greater force to tapes of private Presidential conversations than to Presidential papers.

If release of the tapes would settle the central questions at issue in the Watergate inquiries, then their disclosure might serve a substantial public interest that would have to be weighed very heavily against the negatives of disclosure.

The fact is that the tapes would not finally settle the central issues before your Committee. Before their existence became publicly known, I personally listened to a number of them. The tapes are entirely consistent with what I know to be the truth and what I have stated to be the truth. However, as in any verbatim recording of informal conversations, they contain comments that persons with different perspectives and motivations would inevitably interpret in different ways. Furthermore, there are inseparably interspersed in them a great many very frank and very private comments, on a wide range of issues and individuals, wholly extraneous to the Committee's inquiry. Even more important, the tapes could be accurately understood or interpreted only by reference to an enormous number of other documents and tapes, so that to open them at all would begin an endless process of disclosure and explanation of private Presidential records totally unrelated to Watergate, and highly confidential in nature. They are the clearest possible example of why Presidential documents must be kept confidential.

Accordingly, the tapes, which have been under my sole personal control, must remain so. None has been transcribed or made public and none will be.

On May 22nd I described my knowledge of the Watergate matter and its aftermath in categorical and unambiguous terms that I know to be true. In my letter of July 6th, I informed you that at an appropriate time during the hearings I intend to address publicly the subjects you are considering. I still intend to do so and in a way that preserves the Constitutional principle of separation of powers, and thus serves the interests not just of the Congress or the President, but of the people.

On July 23, 1973—the same day that they learned that Nixon had refused to honor their request to turn over the White House tape recordings—Senator Ervin and Senator Howard Baker (Republican-Tennessee), the vice chairman of the committee, issued public statements criticizing Nixon's decision. The following are excerpts from those statements.

Senator Ervin's Statement

This is a rather remarkable letter about the tapes. If you will notice, the President says he has heard the tapes or some of them, and they sustain his position. But he says he's not going to let anybody else hear them for fear they might draw a different conclusion.

In other words, the President says that they are susceptible of, the way I construe it, two different interpretations, one favorable to his aides and one not favorable to his aides.

I deeply regret this action of the committee [voting to issue subpoenas of the White House tapes and records]. I have very different ideas of separation of powers from those expressed by the President. If such a thing as executive privilege is created by the doctrine of separation of powers, it has these attributes. First, if it exists at all, it only exists in connection with official duties.

Second, under no circumstances can it be involved in either alleged illegal activities or political campaign activities.

I am certain that the doctrine of separation of powers does not impose upon any President either the duty or the power to undertake to separate a congressional committee from access to the truth concerning alleged criminal activities.

I was in hopes that the President would accede to the request of this committee for these tapes and these papers.

I love my country. I venerate the office of the President, and I have the best wishes for the success of the … present incumbent of that office, because he is the only President this country has at this time.

A President not only has constitutional powers which require him to see to it or to take care that the law be faithfully executed, and I think it's his duty under those circumstances to produce information which would either tend to prove or disprove that criminal activities have occurred. But beyond that, the President of the United States, by reason of the fact that he holds the highest office in the gift of the American people, owes an obligation to furnish a high standard of moral leadership to this nation and his constitutional duties, in my opinion, and undoubtedly his duty of affording moral leadership of the country place upon him some obligation under these circumstances.

We have evidence here that during the time the President was running for re-election to the highest office in the gift of the people of this nation that some of his campaign funds were found in the possession of burglars in the headquarters of the opposition political party. And I think that high moral leadership demands that the President make available to this committee any information in the form of tapes or records which will shed some light on that crucial question: How did it happen that burglars were caught in the headquarters of the opposition party with the President's campaign funds in their pockets and in their hotel bedrooms at the time? And I don't think the people of the United States are interested so much in abstruse arguments about the separation of powers or executive privilege as they are in finding the answer to that question.

I deeply regret that this situation has arisen, because I think that the Watergate tragedy is the greatest tragedy this country has ever suffered. I used to think that the Civil War was our country's greatest tragedy, but I do remember that there were some redeeming features in the Civil War in that there was some spirit of sacrifice and heroism displayed on both sides. I see no redeeming features in Watergate.

Senator Baker's Statement

Mr. Chairman, it is difficult for me to express my disappointment that we arrive at the place where at least the leading edge of a confrontation on the question of separation of powers between the Congress and the White House is before us. You have pointed out, I am sure, that this committee has authorized by unanimous vote the issuance of a subpoena *duces tecum* for certain documents and certain portions of the so-called Butterfield tapes relevant to the inquiry of this committee.

As my colleagues on the committee know, I have tried as hard as I know how to find a way around this confrontation. I have suggested various and several alternative possibilities. Even now, I don't despair of hope that we can find a way to reconcile our differences in the conflict that impends between Congress and the executive department. But I concur with my colleagues on the committee in the evaluation that there was no other practical course of action except to authorize the action which has now been described, and I voted for it and I support it.

I think the material sought by the subpoena *duces tecum* or, more accurately, by the subpoenas *duces tecum,* are essential, if not vital, to the full, thorough inquiry mandated and required by this committee.

I shall refrain from expressing my evaluation of the entire situation, that is, the totality of the testimony and the inferences to be drawn from it, until we have heard all of the information, all the witnesses, all the testimony, and examined all the documents that are made available to us. On February 24, 1974, or prior thereto, if the committee files its report at an early date, I will express my conclusions, but not before.

It is my fond hope, however, that when we do finally get to the business of writing a report, that we have all of the available information and that we can in fact write a definitive statement on Watergate—not trying to indict or persecute anyone nor to protect anyone.

The committee has been criticized from time to time for its absence of rules of evidence, the right of confrontation, of cross-examination by counsel, and a number of other legal concepts that we do not have. But we do not have defendants, either, and we are not trying to create defendants. We are trying to find fact, to establish circumstances, to divine the causes, to ascertain the relationships that make up in toto the so-called Watergate affair.

I am unhappy that it is necessary for us to come to the brink of a constitutional confrontation, and although that is a hackneyed phrase, it is an accurate phrase, a constitutional confrontation between the Congress and the White House, a confrontation that has never been resolved in its totality by the courts, a principle and doctrine that has never been fully elaborated and spilled out, in order to fully discharge our obligation as a committee. But I think that is precisely where we are.

I have no criticism of any person. I will not sit in judgment of any person or the conduct of any person until all of the evidence is taken, but I can do no less than try to gain all of the information available on which to base such a conclusion later.

Source: Public Papers of President Richard Nixon, The Richard Nixon Library & Birthplace Foundation, http://www.nixonfoundation.org/Research_Center/1973_pdf_files/1973_0211.pdf; The Sam J. Ervin Papers, Southern Historical Collection, Wilson Library, University of North Carolina at Chapel Hill, NC, http://www.lib.unc.edu/mss/; The Papers of Howard H. Baker, Jr., Special Collections Library of the University of Tennessee, Knoxville, TN, http://www.lib.utk.edu/spcoll/.

Time Magazine Urges President Nixon to Resign

On October 20, 1973, President Richard Nixon fired Special Watergate Prosecutor Archibald Cox and accepted the resignations of Attorney General Elliot Richardson and Deputy Attorney General William D. Ruckelshaus, both of whom had refused to take part in Cox's firing. These events, collectively known as the "Saturday Night Massacre," triggered anger and condemnation across the United States. In the issue of Time *dated November 12, 1973, the magazine's editors published an editorial demanding that Nixon resign the presidency. The statement, titled "The President Should Resign," was the first editorial in the magazine's history. Following is the complete text of the editorial:*

Richard Nixon and the nation have passed a tragic point of no return. It now seems likely that the President will have to give up his office: he has irredeemably lost his moral authority, the confidence of most of the country, and therefore his ability to govern effectively.

The most important decision of Richard Nixon's remarkable career is before him: whether he will give up the presidency rather than do further damage to his country. If he decides to fight to the end, he faces impeachment by the House, for he has indeed failed his obligation under the Constitution to uphold the law. Whether two-thirds of the Senate would vote to convict him cannot be certain. But even if he were to be acquitted, the process would leave him and the country devastated. Events have achieved an alarming momentum: additional facts that would be brought out under subpoena power at an impeachment trial could strike in many unforeseen and dangerous directions.

Moreover, a trial would take at least several months, during which the country would be virtually leaderless. The White House would be paralyzed while the U.S. and the world awaited the outcome. The Republic would doubtless survive. But the wise and patriotic course is for Richard Nixon to resign, sparing the country and himself this agony.

Nixon should of course be succeeded by a Republican. The Republicans did win the presidency last November (not because of Watergate or dirty tricks), and fortunately there seems no disposition among congressional Democrats to try to rewrite the election returns. We assume and hope that Congress will speedily confirm Gerald Ford's nomination as Vice President. If

---

Nixon did leave office before this confirmation and Speaker Carl Albert became president, there is good reason to think that Albert would resign as long as Ford was confirmed.

Gerald Ford would be an unmistakable improvement over the grievously wounded Nixon. Barring some unforeseen revelations, Ford has the immense asset of a corruption-free reputation. He has a solid if unimaginative record in domestic policy, stands somewhere near the American center, and is greatly liked and respected on Capital Hill. In foreign affairs, he is obviously inexperienced, but other Presidents have risen above such limitations, as the example of Harry Truman demonstrates. With Henry Kissinger's help, Ford should be able to carry on the basically sound Nixon policies. He would have one overriding advantage in dealing with foreign powers: their certainty that Ford would be in the White House for at least three more years. Nixon's great skills in foreign affairs are now alarmingly offset by the uncertainties about his future and his patent loss of power at home.

It was just one year ago this week that Richard Nixon was celebrating his fabulous electoral sweep and seemed to stand at the very summit of power and opportunity. Hard-core Nixon haters may gloat over his fall from those heights; for most Americans it is a matter of profound disappointment. The editors of Time Inc., speaking on the editorial page of *Time*'s sister publication *LIFE*, have endorsed Nixon for president three times, in 1960, 1968, and 1972. We did so with acknowledgments that aspects of the Nixon record and temperament were troubling, but we believed that his strengths of intellect and experience and his instinct for political leadership equipped him well for the office. In endorsing Nixon in 1972, following on his first-term achievements in foreign policy, we expressed a hope that by the end of his second term we could "salute him as a great President." Thus, we come with deep reluctance to our conclusion that he must leave office. We consider the situation so unprecedented, the issue so crucial to the country, that we publish this first editorial in *Time*'s 50-year history.

In the almost daily rush of revelations, it is not easy for the numbed citizen to keep in mind the full enormity of "Watergate." Despite ample instances of past Government corruption, nothing can be found in U.S. history even remotely approaching the skein of events that the word Watergate no longer defines or contains. A Vice President, twice personally chosen by Nixon, forced to resign to escape jail. A former Attorney General and intimate advisor to Nixon under indictment. Another former Cabinet member under indictment. One of the two most powerful presidential aides under indictment. Six other White House aides or Administration officials indicted, convicted or having pleaded guilty; seven more fired or resigned. Most of them shown to have been either in charge of, or aware of, illegal operations. The whole White House pervaded by an atmosphere of aggressive amorality—amorality almost raised to a creed. A ruthless determination to hide as much of this as possible from the public and investigators.

The question that once seemed so important—Did the President know about the cover-up?—was always somewhat beside the point. Whatever he knew or did not know, he must be held accountable for the actions of his top aides and the standards he established. To the extent that the question had meaning, it was almost impossible from the start to answer it in the President's favor: the men involved were too close to him to make his ignorance plausible; after initial indignant denials, each of his later explanations gradually admitted more knowledge, thereby conceding each previous explanation to have been at least partly false. One cannot think of any organization, public or private—including some dictatorships—where a Chief Executive could survive in office after such a performance.

The catalogue of the President's involvement in illegal or grossly improper acts has become all too familiar. He approved the so-called Huston plan, which permitted illegal means (including burglary) to combat radicals. He established the "plumbers" unit, ostensibly to plug leaks, and it used illegal methods (wiretaps, forgery) to embarrass or spy on political foes. He impeded an investigation of the plumbers on specious national-security grounds while his aides tried to use the CIA and FBI to help the cover-up. He had a job offer (chief of the FBI) dangled before the judge presiding over the trial of Daniel Ellsberg. He withheld knowledge of the Ellsberg-psychiatrist burglary from that judge for at least a month. His aides offered Executive clemency to some of the Watergate defendants; others, including his personal lawyer, used campaign contributions for payments to Watergate defendants.

President Nixon's most recent actions come as a staggering climax to all that went before. We devoutly hope that it *is* the climax. When he originally refused to hand over the White House tapes either to the Senate Watergate committee or to Special Prosecutor Archibald Cox, his argument for the confidentiality of the President's deliberations certainly deserved consideration. Then the court narrowed the issue in such a way that confidentiality could be largely safeguarded; only the judge was to hear the tapes, and only for the purpose of deciding whether any parts were potential evidence in the cases arising from Watergate. If the President had wanted to contest this ruling, he had a clear opportunity to have the matter settled in the Supreme Court, by whose decision he had earlier said that he would abide.

Instead, the President and his lawyer worked out the "compromise" under which summaries would be provided (they would not hold up as evidence in court), and Special Prosecutor Archibald Cox was to be forbidden any further recourse to the courts in seeking presidential papers. Cox sensibly refused, and was promptly fired in flagrant violation of the President's pledge to the Senate, through then-Attorney General-designate Richardson, that Cox would be independent and could be dismissed only for gross improprieties. That brought on the resignation of Richardson and the dismissal of his principal assistant, honorable men who both refused to carry out the President's order to fire Cox. After an outpouring of indignation from Congress and country, which saw Nixon as defying the courts and setting himself above the law, came the President's abrupt reversal and his decision to hand the tapes to the court after all. And only a few days ago, there was the sudden claim that two crucial tapes do not exist.

Now the President has found a new Attorney General and a new special prosecutor, equipped with not quite convincing promises of independence. Both are reputable men, but it seems to us that these appointments or even the possible appointment of a prosecutor by the court, can no longer clear away the hopeless miasma of deceit and suspicion.

The right of free men to choose their leaders is precious and rare in a world mainly ruled by authoritarian governments. It is the genius of the American Constitution that it combines stability with liberty; it does so in part by fixing a term for the Chief Executive and largely protecting him from the caprices of parliamentary governments. An American President must be given the widest freedom of action, the utmost tolerance, the most generous benefit of every doubt. It is a system that has served us well.

A President's Gallup rating can fluctuate as much as the Dow Jones. He may push unpopular programs or oppose popular ones. Being a political as well as a national leader, he may dissemble within more or less accepted political limits. His Administration may be touched by corruption, provided that he does not condone it. He may make mistakes, many of them. He may fight the other branches of Government, for this is sometimes necessary to get things done. None of these matters—especially since they are always subject to partisan interpretation—are sufficient in themselves to justify the removal of a President.

Yet there is a limit beyond which even such "permissible" offenses, even such instances of "mere" misgovernment, become intolerable. And the situation changes fundamentally when the effect of the President's actions and the actions of his appointees is to subvert the constitutional system itself. He then betrays his formal oath of office and his informal compact with the people.

There are legitimate fears about the precedent that would be set by the President's resignation or impeachment. In two centuries, no American President has been removed from office other than by death or the voters' will. Once the spell is broken, would it become too easy for political opponents of any future President to oust him? We think not. Watergate is unique. In fact, the really dangerous precedent would be the opposite: to allow a President with Nixon's record to continue in office. This would be a terrible circumstance to lodge in our history, a terrible thing to explain to our children and their children.

In recent decades, the American presidency has assumed an almost sacrosanct aura. It is time to remember that quite literally, and not as a flourish of speech, the sovereign in America is not the President but the people. It is true that the people elect him, which gives him a unique mandate, but to conclude from this that a President must be preserved in all circumstances, at any cost, is the first unwitting step toward dictatorship.

As Watergate and related events emerged in congressional hearings and in the press, many patriotic Americans were nagged by a sense of disproportion. Crookedness and corner cutting? Yes. Crimes? No doubt—but after all, as the phrase went, "No one was killed." How could these acts, however shady or offensive, be weighed against the life-and-death responsibilities of the President? This rationalization will not stand; a President's "big decisions" cannot be put into a compartment separate from his other actions, his total behavior. His integrity and trustworthiness are perhaps the most important facts about him to his country and to the world. And these Nixon has destroyed.

The nightmare of uncertainty must be ended. A fresh start must be made. Some at home and abroad might see in the President's resignation a sign of American weakness and failure. It would be a sign of the very opposite. It would show strength and health. It would show the ability of a badly infected political system to cleanse itself. It would show the true power of popular government under law in America.

Source: "The President Should Resign." *Time,* November 12, 1973.

Judge Sirica Listens to the First Wave of Watergate Tapes

After months of battle in the courts and the arena of public opinion, the Nixon White House turned seven subpoenaed Watergate tapes over to Federal Judge John Sirica for his review in December 1973. It was Sirica's responsibility to determine whether executive privilege could be invoked for any portions of the tapes. He eventually upheld claims of executive privilege on portions of three tapes; the remainder he sent on to Special Prosecutor Leon Jaworski and the grand jury investigating Watergate. In the following excerpt from his 1979 memoir To Set the Record Straight, *Sirica recalls listening to the tapes for the first time with law clerk Todd Christofferson:*

On Saturday, December 8, Todd and I began listening to the tapes. At first, it was a stunning experience. We had sequestered ourselves in the small jury room off my courtroom. This was the very room in which the jurors, after discussing the case around the large, oak conference table that occupies most of the floor space, had found the break-in defendants guilty. Painted government green, this room has no distractions at all—no windows and only one door. It is virtually soundproof, and we were shut away from the rest of the world. The recorder was set up on a scarred wooden table next to one wall. Paper was stuffed under the record key to prevent accidental erasure. As we sat there alone, headphones on, the sounds of the president and his lieutenants seemed to put them in the same little room with us....

At first, we were shocked by the frequent profanity. I came up the hard way, and the language was far from unfamiliar to me. But the shock, for me at least, was the contrast between the coarse, private Nixon speech and the utterly correct public Nixon speech I had heard so often. Public figures often present this contrast, I know, but Nixon's swearing was somehow more surprising than that of other men I had heard relax their speaking standards in private. As I first realized the barnyard quality of his conversations, I couldn't help remembering the rather self-righteous attack Nixon had made, during the 1960 television debates with John F. Kennedy, on Harry Truman's salty language.

That Saturday, Todd and I worked our way through two tapes—one of a conversation on March 13, 1973, between the president, John Dean, and H. R. Haldeman, in the Oval Office, and one of a meeting on March 22, 1973, involving the president, Dean, Ehrlichman, Haldeman, and Mitchell, in the president's office in the Executive Office Building. The March 13 tape included a very blunt discussion of Senator Lowell Weicker of Connecticut (a Republican who had charged Haldeman with some responsibility for the Watergate mess), the president's advice to Haldeman to sue Weicker, some talk about a scheme to hire Charles Colson as an unpaid consultant so that he would have the protection of executive privilege if called to testify before the Senate Watergate committee, and a discussion of dumping L. Patrick Gray as the nominee to head the FBI.

The March 22 meeting focused on a plan to have Dean write a report that would give the appearance of being a thorough explanation of the White House role in the Watergate affair, but would in fact omit damaging information....

What was most striking about these tapes was the total absence of any desire by the president to clean up the mess. His public statements for nearly a year had emphasized his own insistence, once Dean had informed him of the facts on March 21, on rooting out the wrongdoers in the White House. By the time I heard the tapes, I was not surprised that Nixon was more intent on maintaining the cover-up than on getting to the bottom of the case. But as I actually listened to him coaching his aides on the cover-up, and realized that he was displaying no outrage, not even the normal anger that one would expect from a politician whose aides have gotten him into trouble, I found the whole thing disgusting. A lifetime of dealing with the criminal law, of watching a parade of people who had robbed, stolen, killed, raped, and deceived others, had not hardened me enough to hear with equanimity the low political scheming that was being played back to me from the White House offices. I had given lectures on the virtues and privileges of American citizenship to thousands of people during naturalization proceedings. I had praised our form of government to these new citizens. It was one of the most disillusioning experiences of my life to have to listen now to what had gone on at the highest levels of the government of the United States of America. I'll never forget hearing the president tell his aides on the March 22 tape, "And, uh, for that reason, I am perfectly willing to—I don't give a shit what happens. I want you all to stonewall it, let them plead the Fifth Amendment, cover-up or anything else, if it'll save it—save the plan."

From that moment on, there was no longer any doubt in my mind that there had been a conspiracy to obstruct justice operating inside the White House. I thought back over the months of legal arguments over the tapes, the high-sounding claims of executive privilege, the pleas to protect the ability of the president to function in private, and thanked God that I had ruled as I did. It all seemed so hollow after hearing the president calling for a stone wall, a cover-up, to protect himself and his highest aides from criminal prosecution and from political disaster. I had taken the arguments about executive privilege very seriously indeed. Now they seemed just another stage of the cover-up. Nixon, it was clear from his own words, was deeply involved in the whole rotten mess. It was impossible to say, right then, just what this tape would mean for Nixon himself. But added to the testimony of Dean, Magruder, and others, these tapes, it seemed to me, would clinch the indictment of Haldeman, Mitchell, and Ehrlichman. I left the office that weekend more depressed than ever.

But I really hadn't heard the worst of it. On Monday, Todd again went to the big, gray file-sale. He took out the March 21 tape and set it up on the recorder in the jury room. Again, he stuffed paper under the record key to prevent any accidental erasures. The two of us again closed the door, put on our earphones, and began listening to the president of the United States and his private responses to the Watergate problem. This was the tape of the critical meeting with John Dean, the meeting about which Dean had testified so thoroughly before the Senate committee the previous summer....

Whatever Nixon had known before March 21 (his public statements had stressed that he first learned of the cover-up at this meeting with Dean, but this position was of course destroyed by the other tapes), he certain knew everything after the meeting, which took nearly two hours. Dean, frightened that the whole scheme was falling apart, had come to Nixon to lay out all the facts and seek the president's advice on what to do next. The most critical problem that Dean laid before Nixon was the difficulty in raising money to keep the defendants in the break-in case quiet. Dean's recitation of the facts of the Watergate cover-up was almost as complete as that of a prosecutor laying out the theory of his case before a jury. Again, I noticed the absence of shock or surprise or anger in Nixon's responses as the details of the conspiracy were presented by Dean....

The tape not only gave the lie to the president's public contention that after the March 21 meeting with Dean he had begun to try to root out the conspirators in the White House, it put Nixon at the head of the conspiracy to obstruct justice, as far as I was concerned. I had heard for myself the president of the United States order a pay-off to a criminal defendant to buy his silence....

154

Neither Todd nor I said much afterward. I did note to Todd that the tape certainly provided corroboration for Dean's testimony. But it did much more. It provided indisputable evidence, as far as I could tell, of the president's engaging in a criminal act.

I had really hoped the president himself would not be so involved, that he would survive this scandal. After all, I had campaigned for him twice when he ran with President Eisenhower, in 1952 and 1956. I remembered the speeches I had made in 1952, shouting from the hilltops about the scandals in the Truman administration, urging the election of Ike and Nixon to clean up the government. Not that I had had a big role in their election, but I had believed in them. I had spoken out for them. After listening to Nixon on tape, I felt foolish. I am a Republican. As angry as I had been at Nixon over the past months, as much as I had thought he was following the wrong course in opposing the release of the tapes, I still, in my heart, didn't want to hear what Todd and I had just listened to. We had voted for him in 1968 and again in 1972.

Todd and I left the courthouse that evening tired and dispirited. I remembered Nixon saying earlier in the fall, "I am not a crook." Well, I felt we did have a dishonest man in the White House, a president who had violated the law, who had conspired to obstruct the very laws he was sworn to uphold. It was a frightening thing to know.

Source: Sirica, John. *To Set the Record Straight: The Break-In, the Tapes, the Conspirators, and the Pardon.* New York: Norton, 1979.

Representative Barbara Jordan's Speech on Constitutional Law, July 25, 1974

On July 24, 1974, after 14 months of investigations, the U.S. House of Representatives' House Judiciary Committee prepared to vote on whether or not to recommend impeachment. Before the formal vote took place, each committee member was permitted a 15-minute statement, with order determined by seniority.

Early on the morning of July 25, 1974, freshman Democratic Representative Barbara Jordan of Texas finally had the opportunity to deliver her remarks. Only two years earlier, she had become the first African-American lawmaker to represent a previously Confederate state in the U.S. Congress. But she had already gained a reputation in Washington, D.C., as a conscientious and independent-minded politician.

Jordan began her statement a little after 2 a.m., when most Americans were asleep in bed. Yet her speech garnered a great deal of attention in subsequent days, including repeated airings of excerpts on television and radio programs. Jordan's statement of deep and abiding faith in the Constitution was widely regarded as a timely reminder to committee members of their solemn obligation to put political considerations aside when weighing vital matters of constitutional law.

M r. Chairman:

I join in thanking you for giving the junior members of this committee the glorious opportunity of sharing the pain of this inquiry. Mr. Chairman, you are a strong man and it has not been easy but we have tried as best we can to give you as much assistance as possible.

Earlier today, we heard the beginning of the Preamble to the Constitution of the United States, "We, the people." It is a very eloquent beginning. But when the document was completed on the seventeenth of September 1787 I was not included in that "We, the people." I felt somehow for many years that George Washington and Alexander Hamilton just left me out by mistake. But through the process of amendment, interpretation and court decision I have finally been included in "We, the people."

Today, I am an inquisitor; I believe hyperbole would not be fictional and would not overstate the solemnness that I feel right now. My faith in the Constitution is whole, it is complete, it is total. I am not going to sit here and be an idle spectator to the diminution, the subversion, the destruction of the Constitution....

The subject of its jurisdiction are those offenses which proceed from the misconduct of public men. That is what we are talking about. In other words, the jurisdiction comes from the abuse or violation of some public trust. It is wrong, I suggest, it is a misreading of the Constitution, for any member here to assert that for a member to vote for an article of impeachment means that that member must be convinced that the President should be removed from office.

The Constitution doesn't say that. The powers relating to impeachment are an essential check in the hands of this body, the legislature, against and upon the encroachment of the Executive [Branch]. In establishing the division between the two branches of the legislature, the House and the Senate, assigning to the one the right to accuse and the other the right to judge, the framers of the Constitution were very astute. They did not make the accusers and the judges the same person.

We know the nature of impeachment. We have been talking about it awhile now. It is chiefly designed for the President and his high ministers to somehow be called into account. It is designed to "bridle" the Executive if he engages in excesses. It is designed as a method of national inquest into the conduct of public men. The framers confined in the Congress the power, if need be, to remove the President in order to strike a delicate balance between a President swollen with power and grown tyrannical and preservation of the independence of the Executive. The nature of impeachment is a narrowly channeled exception to the separation of powers maxim; the federal convention of 1787 said that. It limited impeachment to high crimes and misdemeanors and discounted and opposed the term "maladministration." "It [impeachment] is to be used only for great misdemeanors," so it was said in the North Carolina ratification convention. And in the Virginia ratification convention: "We need one branch to check the others."

The North Carolina ratification convention: "No one need to be afraid that officers who commit oppression will pass with immunity."

"Prosecutions of impeachments will seldom fail to agitate the passions of the whole community," said Hamilton in the *Federalist Papers*, number 65. "And to divide it into parties more or less friendly or inimical to the accused." I do not mean political parties in that sense.

The drawing of political lines goes to the motivation behind impeachment; but impeachment must proceed within the confines of the constitutional term, "high crimes and misdemeanors."

Of the impeachment process, it was Woodrow Wilson who said that "nothing short of the grossest offenses against the plainest law of the land will suffice to give them speed and effectiveness. Indignation so great as to overgrow party interest may secure a conviction; but nothing else can."

Common sense would be revolted if we engaged upon this process for petty reasons. Congress has a lot to do: Appropriations, tax reform, health insurance, campaign finance reform, housing, environmental protection, energy sufficiency, mass transportation. Pettiness cannot be allowed to stand in the face of such overwhelming problems. So today we are not being petty. We are trying to be big, because the task we have before us is a big one.

This morning, in a discussion of the evidence, we were told that the evidence which purports to support the allegation of misuse of the CIA by the President is thin. We are told that that evidence is insufficient. What that recital of the evidence this morning did not include is what the President did know on June 23, 1972. The President did know that it was Republican money, that it was money from the Committee for the Re-Election of the President, which was found in the possession of one of the burglars arrested on June 17.

What the President did know on June 23 was the prior activities of E. Howard Hunt, which included his participation in the break-in of Daniel Ellsberg's psychiatrist, which included ... Howard Hunt's fabrication of cables designed to discredit the Kennedy Administration.

We were further cautioned today that perhaps these proceedings ought to be delayed because certainly there would be new evidence forthcoming from the President of the United States. There has not even been an obfuscated indication that this committee would receive any additional materials from the President. The committee subpoena [for numerous Watergate tapes] is outstanding and if the President wants to supply that material, the committee sits here. The fact is that on yesterday, the American people waited with great anxiety for eight hours, not knowing whether their President would obey an order of the Supreme Court of the United States.

At this point, I would like to juxtapose a few of the impeachment criteria with some of the President's actions.

158

Impeachment criteria: James Madison, from the Virginia ratification convention—"If the president be connected in any suspicious manner with any person and there is grounds to believe that he will shelter him, he may be impeached."

We have heard time and time again that the evidence reflects payment to the defendants of money. The President had knowledge that these funds were being paid and that these were funds collected for the 1972 presidential campaign. We know that the President met with Mr. Henry Peterson twenty-seven times to discuss matters related to Watergate, and immediately thereafter met with the very persons who were implicated in the information Mr. Peterson was receiving and transmitting to the President. The words are, "If the President be connected in any suspicious manner with any person and there be grounds to believe that he will shelter that person, he may be impeached."

Justice [Joseph] Story: "Impeachment is intended for occasional and extraordinary cases where a superior power acting for the whole people is put into operation to protect their rights and rescue their liberties from violations."

We know about the Huston Plan. We know about the break-in of the psychiatrist's office. We know that there was absolute, complete direction in August 1971 when the President instructed Ehrlichman to "do whatever is necessary." This instruction led to a surreptitious entry into Dr. Fielding's office. "Protect their rights." "Rescue their liberties from violation."

The South Carolina ratification convention impeachment criteria: Those are impeachable "who behave amiss or betray their public trust."

Beginning shortly after the Watergate break-in and continuing to the present time, the President has engaged in a series of public statements and actions designed to thwart the lawful investigation by government prosecutors. Moreover, the President has made public announcements and assertions bearing on the Watergate case which the evidence will show he knew to be false. These assertions, false assertions; impeachable, those who misbehave. Those who "behave amiss or betray their public trust."

James Madison, again at the constitutional convention: "A President is impeachable if he attempts to subvert the Constitution."

The Constitution charges the President with the task of taking care that the laws be faithfully executed, and yet the President has counseled his aides to commit perjury, willfully disregarded the secrecy of grand jury proceedings, concealed surreptitious entry, attempted to compromise a federal judge while publicly displaying his cooperation with the process of criminal justice. "A president is impeachable if he attempts to subvert the Constitution."

If the impeachment provision in the Constitution of the United States will not reach the offenses charged here, then perhaps that eighteenth century Constitution should be abandoned to a twentieth-century paper shredder.

Has the President committed offenses and planned and directed and acquiesced in a course of conduct which the Constitution will not tolerate? This is the question. We know that. We know the question.

We should now forthwith proceed to answer the question.

It is reason, and not passion, which must guide our deliberations, guide our debate, and guide our decision.

Mr. Chairman, I yield back the balance of my time.

Source: Barbara Jordan National Forum on Public Policy presented by the Lyndon R. Johnson School of Public Affairs, http://www.utexas.edu/lbj/barbarajordanforum/PDFs/ PDF_Opening%20Statement%20to%20the%20House%20Judiciary%20Committee.pdf

House Judiciary Committee Resolution to Impeach President Nixon

In July 1974 the Judiciary Committee of the U.S. House of Representatives held televised proceedings chaired by Democratic Representative Peter Rodino of New Jersey. In late July the committee approved three articles of impeachment against President Richard Nixon in connection with the Watergate scandal. This excerpt from the committee's final report to the House of Representatives details each of the three articles of impeachment.

The committee on the Judiciary, to whom was referred the consideration of recommendations concerning the exercise of the constitutional power to impeach Richard M. Nixon, President of the United States, having considered the same, reports thereon pursuant to Il. Re. 803 as follows and recommends that the House exercise its constitutional power to impeach Richard M. Nixon, President of the United States, and that articles of impeachment be exhibited to the Senate as follows:

RESOLUTION

Impeaching Richard M. Nixon, President of the United States, of high crimes and misdemeanors.

Resolved, That Richard M. Nixon, President of the United States, is impeached for high crimes and misdemeanors, and that the following articles of impeachment be exhibited to the Senate:

Articles of impeachment exhibited by the House of Representatives of the United States of America in the name of itself and of all of the people of the United States of America, against Richard M. Nixon, President of the United States of America, in maintenance and support of its impeachment against him for high crimes and misdemeanors.

ARTICLE I

In his conduct of the office of President of the United States, Richard M. Nixon, in violation of his constitutional oath faithfully to execute the office of President of the United States and, to the best of his ability, preserve, protect, and defend the Constitution of the United States, and in violation of his constitutional duty to take care that the laws be faithfully executed, has prevented, obstructed, and impeded the administration of justice, in that:

161

On June 17, 1972, and prior thereto, agents of the Committee for the Re-election of the President committed unlawful entry of the headquarters of the Democratic National Committee in Washington, District of Columbia, for the purpose of securing political intelligence. Subsequent thereto, Richard M. Nixon, using the powers of his high office, engaged personally and through his subordinates and agents, in a course of conduct or plan designed to delay, impede, and obstruct the investigation of such unlawful entry; to cover up, conceal and protect those responsible; and to conceal the existence and scope of other unlawful covert activities.

The means used to implement this course of conduct or plan included one or more of the following:

1. making or causing to be made false or misleading statements to lawfully authorized investigative officers and employees of the United States;

2. withholding relevant and material evidence or information from lawfully authorized investigative officers and employees of the United States;

3. approving, condoning, acquiescing in, and counseling witnesses with respect to the giving of false or misleading statements to lawfully authorized investigative officers and employees of the United States and false or misleading testimony in duly instituted judicial and congressional proceedings.

4. interfering or endeavoring to interfere with the conduct of investigations by the Department of Justice of the United States, the Federal Bureau of Investigation, the Office of Watergate Special Prosecution Force, and Congressional Committees;

5. approving, condoning, and acquiescing in, the surreptitious payment of substantial sums of money for the purpose of obtaining the silence or influencing the testimony of witnesses, potential witnesses or individuals who participated in such unlawful entry and other illegal activities;

6. endeavoring to misuse the Central Intelligence Agency, an agency of the United States;

7. disseminating information received from officers of the Department of Justice of the United States to subjects of investigations conducted by lawfully authorized investigative officers and

employees of the United States, for the purpose of aiding and assisting such subjects in their attempts to avoid criminal liability;

8. making false or misleading public statements for the purpose of deceiving the people of the United States into believing that a thorough and complete investigation has been conducted with respect to allegations of misconduct on the parts of personnel of the executive branch of the United States and personnel of the Committee for the Re-election of the President and that there was no involvement of such personnel in such misconduct; or

9. endeavoring to cause prospective defendants, and individuals duly tried and convicted, to expect favored treatment and considerations in return for their silence or false testimony, or rewarding individuals for their silence or false testimony.

In all of this, Richard M. Nixon has acted in a manner contrary to his trust as President and subversive of constitutional government, to the great prejudice of the cause of law and justice and to the manifest injury of the people of the United States.

Wherefore Richard M. Nixon, by such conduct, warrants impeachment and trial and removal from office.

ARTICLE II

Using the powers of the office of President of the United States, Richard M. Nixon, in violation of his constitutional oath faithfully to execute the office of President of the United States and, to the best of his ability, preserve, protect, and defend the Constitution of the United States, and in disregard of his constitutional duty to take care that the laws be faithfully executed, has repeatedly engaged in conduct violating the constitutional rights of citizens, impairing the due and proper administration of justice and the conduct of lawful inquiries, or contravening the laws governing agencies of the executive branch and the purposes of these agencies.

This conduct has included one or more of the following:

1. He has, acting personally and through his subordinates and agents, endeavored to obtain from the Internal Revenue Service, in violation of the constitutional rights of citizens, confidential information contained in income tax returns for purposes not

authorized by law, and to cause, in violation of the constitutional rights of citizens, income tax audits or other income tax investigations to be initiated or conducted in a discriminatory manner.

2. He misused the Federal Bureau of Investigation, the Secret Service, and other executive personnel, in violation or disregard of the constitutional rights of citizens, by directing or authorizing such agencies or personnel to conduct or continue electronic surveillance or other investigations for purposes unrelated to national security, the enforcement of laws, or any other lawful function of his office; and he did direct the concealment of certain records made by the Federal Bureau of Investigation of electronic surveillance.

3. He has, acting personally and through his subordinates and agents, in violation or disregard of the constitutional rights of citizens, authorized and permitted to be maintained a secret investigative unit within the office of the President, financed in part with money derived from campaign contributions, which unlawfully utilized resources of the Central Intelligence Agency, engaged in covert and unlawful activities, and attempted to prejudice the constitutional right of an accused to a fair trial.

4. He has failed to take care that the laws were faithfully executed by failing to act when he knew or had reason to know that his close subordinates endeavored to impede and frustrate lawful inquires by duly constituted executive, judicial, and legislative entities concerning the unlawful entry into the headquarters of the Democratic National Committee, and the cover up thereof, and concerning other unlawful activities, including those related to the confirmation of Richard Kleindienst as Attorney General of the United States, the electronic surveillance of private citizens, the break-in into the offices of Dr. Lewis Fielding, and the campaign financing practices of the Committee to Re-elect the President.

5. In disregard of the rule of law, he knowingly misused the executive power by interfering with agencies of the executive branch, including the Federal Bureau of Investigation, the Criminal Division, and the Office of Watergate Special Prosecution Force, of the Department of Justice, and the Central Intelligence Agency, in violation of his duty to take care that the laws be faithfully executed.

In all of this, Richard M. Nixon has acted in a manner contrary to his trust as President and subversive of constitutional government, to the great prejudice of the cause of law and justice and to the manifest injury of the people of the United States.

Wherefore Richard M. Nixon, by such conduct, warrants impeachment and removal from office.

ARTICLE III

In his conduct of the office of President of the United States, Richard M. Nixon, contrary to his oath faithfully to execute the office of President of the United States and, to the best of his ability, preserve, protect, and defend the Constitution of the United States, and in violation of his constitutional duty to take care that the laws be faithfully executed, has failed without lawful cause or excuse to produce papers and things as directed by duly authorized subpoenas issued by the Committee on the Judiciary of the House of Representatives on April 11, 1974, May 30, 1974, and June 24, 1974, and willfully disobeyed such subpoeanas. The subpoenaed papers and things were deemed necessary by the committee in order to resolve by direct evidence fundamental, factual questions relating to Presidential direction, knowledge, or approval of actions demonstrated by other evidence to be substantial grounds for impeachment of the President. In refusing to produce these papers and things, Richard M. Nixon, substituting his judgment as to what materials were necessary for the inquiry, interposed the powers of the Presidency against the lawful subpoenas of the House of Representatives, thereby assuming to himself functions and judgments necessary to the exercise of the sole power of impeachment vested by the Constitution in the House of Representatives.

In all of this, Richard M. Nixon has acted in a manner contrary to his trust as President and subversive of constitutional government, to the great prejudice of the cause of law and justice, and to the manifest injury of the people of the United States.

Wherefore Richard M. Nixon, by such conduct, warrants impeachment and trial and removal from office.

Source: U.S. House of Representatives. Committee on the Judiciary. *Impeachment of Richard M. Nixon, President of the United States; The Final Report of the Committee on the Judiciary, House of Representatives.* New York: Viking, 1975.

President Nixon's Resignation Speech

On August 8, 1974, President Richard M. Nixon announced his intention to resign from office, effective at noon the following day, in a nationally televised address to the nation. Following is the full text of his statement of resignation.

Good evening.

This is the 37th time I have spoken to you from this office in which so many decisions have been made that shape the history of this nation. Each time I have done so to discuss with you some matters that I believe affected the national interest.

In all the decisions I have made in my public life I have always tried to do what was best for the nation. Throughout the long and difficult period of Watergate, I have felt it was my duty to persevere; to make every possible effort to complete the term of office to which you elected me.

In the past few days, however, it has become evident to me that I no longer have a strong enough political base in the Congress to justify continuing that effort. As long as there was such a base, I felt strongly that it was necessary to see the constitutional process through to its conclusion; that to do otherwise would be unfaithful to the spirit of that deliberately difficult process, and a dangerously destabilizing precedent for the future.

But with the disappearance of that base, I now believe that the constitutional purpose has been served. And there is no longer a need for the process to be prolonged.

I would have preferred to carry through to the finish whatever the personal agony it would have involved, and my family unanimously urged me to do so.

But the interests of the nation must always come before any personal considerations. From the discussions I have had with Congressional and other leaders I have concluded that because of the Watergate matter I might not have the support of the Congress that I would consider necessary to back the very difficult decisions and carry out the duties of this office in the way the interests of the nation will require.

I have never been a quitter.

To leave office before my term is completed is abhorrent to every instinct in my body. But as President I must put the interests of America first.

America needs a full-time President and a full-time Congress, particularly at this time with problems we face at home and abroad. To continue to fight through the months ahead for my personal vindication would almost totally absorb the time and attention of both the President and the Congress in a period when our entire focus should be on the great issues of peace abroad and prosperity without inflation at home.

Therefore, I shall resign the Presidency effective at noon tomorrow. Vice President Ford will be sworn in as President at that hour in this office.

As I recall the high hopes for America with which we began this second term, I feel a great sadness that I will not be here in this office working on your behalf to achieve those hopes in the next two and a half years.

But in turning over direction of the government to Vice President Ford I know, as I told the nation when I nominated him for that office 10 months ago, that the leadership of America will be in good hands.

In passing this office to the Vice President I also do so with the profound sense of the weight of responsibility that will fall on his shoulders tomorrow, and therefore of the understanding, the patience, the cooperation he will need from all Americans.

As he assumes that responsibility he will deserve the help and the support of all of us. As we look to the future, the first essential is to begin healing the wounds of this nation. To put the bitterness and division of the recent past behind us and to rediscover those shared ideals that lie at the heart of our strength and unity as a great nation and as a free people. By taking this action, I hope that I will have hastened the start of that process of healing which is so desperately needed in America.

I regret deeply any injuries that may have been done in the course of the events that led to this decision. I would say only that if some of my judgments were wrong—and some were wrong—they were made in what I believed at the time to be the best interests of the nation.

To those who have stood with me during these past difficult months, to my family, my friends, the many others who've joined in supporting my cause because they believed it was right, I will be eternally grateful for your support.

And to those who have not felt able to give me your support, let me say I leave with no bitterness toward those who have opposed me, because all of us in the final analysis have been concerned with the good of the country, however our judgments might differ.

So let us all now join together in affirming that common commitment and in helping our new President succeed for the benefit of all Americans.

I shall leave this office with regret at not completing my term but with gratitude for the privilege of serving as your President for the past five and a half years. These years have been a momentous time in the history of our nation and the world. They have been a time of achievement in which we can all be proud—achievements that represent that shared efforts of the Administration, the Congress and the people. But the challenges ahead are equally great.

And they, too, will require the support and the efforts of a Congress and the people, working in cooperation with the new Administration.

We have ended America's longest war. But in the work of securing a lasting peace in the world, the goals ahead are even more far-reaching and more difficult. We must complete a structure of peace, so that it will be said of this generation—our generation of Americans—by the people of all nations, not only that we ended one war but that we prevented future wars.

We have unlocked the doors that for a quarter of a century stood between the United States and the People's Republic of China. We must now insure that the one-quarter of the world's people who live in the People's Republic of China will be and remain, not our enemies, but our friends.

In the Middle East, 100 million people in the Arab countries, many of whom have considered us their enemies for nearly 20 years, now look on us as friends. We must continue to build on that friendship so that peace can settle at last over the Middle East and so that the cradle of civilization will not become its grave.

Together with the Soviet Union we have made the crucial breakthroughs that have begun the process of limiting nuclear arms. But, we must set as our goal, not just limiting, but reducing and finally destroying these terrible weapons so that they cannot destroy civilization. And so that the threat of nuclear war will no longer hang over the world and the people, we have opened a new relationship with the Soviet Union. We must continue to develop and expand that new relationship so that the two strongest nations of the world will live together in cooperation rather than confrontation.

Around the world—in Asia, in Africa, in Latin America, in the Middle East—there are millions of people who live in terrible poverty, even starvation. We must keep as our goal turning away from production for war and expanding production for peace so that people everywhere on this earth can at last look forward, in their children's time if not in our time, to having the necessities for a decent life.

Here in America we are fortunate that most of our people have not only the blessing of liberty but also the means to live full and good, and by the world's standards even abundant, lives. We must press on, however, toward a goal not only of more and better jobs but of full opportunity for every man, and of what we are striving so hard right now to achieve—prosperity without inflation.

For more than a quarter of a century in public life, I have shared in the turbulent history of this era. I have fought for what I believe in. I have tried, to the best of my ability, to discharge those duties and meet those responsibilities that were entrusted to me.

Sometimes I have succeeded, and sometimes I have failed. But always I have taken heart from what Theodore Roosevelt said about the man in the arena, "whose face is marred by dust and sweat and blood, who strives valiantly, who errs and comes short again and again because there is no effort without error and shortcoming, but who does actually strive to do the deed, who knows the great enthusiasms, the great devotions, who spends himself in a worthy cause, who at the best knows in the end the triumphs of high achievements and who at the worst, if he fails, at least fails while daring greatly."

I pledge to you tonight that as long as I have a breath of life in my body, I shall continue in that spirit. I shall continue to work for the great causes to which I have been dedicated throughout my years as a Congressman, a Senator, Vice President, and President, the cause of peace—not just for America but among all nations—prosperity, justice and opportunity for all of our people.

There is one cause above all, to which I have been devoted and to which I shall always be devoted for as long as I live. When I first took the oath of office as President five and a half years ago, I made this sacred commitment: to consecrate my office, my energies and all the wisdom I can summon to the cause of peace among nations.

I've done my very best in all the days since to be true to that pledge. As a result of these efforts, I am confident that the world is a safer place today, not only for the people of America but for the people of all nations, and that all of our children have a better chance than before of living in peace rather than dying in war.

This, more than anything, is what I hoped to achive when I sought the Presidency. This, more than anything, is what I hope will be my legacy to you, to our country, as I leave the Presidency.

To have served in this office is to have felt a very personal sense of kinship with each and every American. In leaving it, I do so with this prayer: May God's grace be with you in all the days ahead.

Source: Richard Nixon Library and Birthplace Foundation, http://www.nixonfoundation. org/Research_Center/1974_pdf_files/1974_0244.pdf

President Nixon's Parting Remarks

On the morning of August 9, 1974, Richard Nixon gathered together various members of his Cabinet, members of the White House staff, and close family and friends in the East Room of the White House. Following his remarks, which were broadcast live on national television and radio, the president and his wife left the White House for Andrews Air Force Base, where they boarded an airplane that took them home to San Clemente, California. They were in mid-flight at noon, when Nixon's resignation took effect and Gerald Ford was sworn in as the new president of the United States. Following is the transcript of Nixon's final public remarks as president:

Members of the Cabinet, members of the White House Staff, all of our friends here:

I think the record should show that this is one of those spontaneous things that we always arrange whenever the President comes in to speak, and it will be so reported in the press, and we don't mind, because they have to call it as they see it.

But on our part, believe me, it is spontaneous.

You are here to say goodbye to us, and we don't have a good word for it in English—the best is *au revoir*. We will see you again.

I just met with the members of the White House staff, you know, those who serve here in the White House day in and day out, and I asked them to do what I ask all of you to do to the extent that you can and, of course, are requested to do so: to serve our next President as you have served me and previous Presidents—because many of you have been here for many years— with devotion and dedication, because this office, great as it is, can only be as great as the men and women who work for and with the President.

This house, for example—I was thinking of it as we walked down this hall, and I was comparing it to some of the great houses of the world that I have been in. This isn't the biggest house. Many, and most, in even smaller countries, are much bigger. This isn't the finest house. Many in Europe, particularly, and in China, Asia, have paintings of great, great value, things that we just don't have here and, probably, will never have until we are 1,000 years old or older.

But this is the best house. It is the best house because it has something far more important than numbers of people who serve, far more important than numbers of rooms or how big it is, far more important than numbers of magnificent pieces of art.

This house has a great heart, and that heart comes from those who serve. I was rather sorry they didn't come down. We said goodbye to them upstairs. But they are really great. And I recall after so many times I have made speeches, and some of them pretty tough, yet, I always come back, or after a hard day—and my days usually have run rather long—I would always get a lift from them, because I might be a little down but they always smiled.

And so it is with you. I look around here, and I see so many on this staff that, you know, I should have been by your offices and shaken hands, and I would love to have talked to you and found out how to run the world—everybody wants to tell the President what to do, and boy, he needs to be told many times—but I just haven't had the time. But I want you to know that each and every one of you, I know, is indispensable to this Government.

I am proud of this Cabinet. I am proud of all the members who have served in our Cabinet. I am proud of our sub-Cabinet. I am proud of our White House Staff. As I pointed out last night, sure, we have done some things wrong in this Administration, and the top man always takes the responsibility, and I have never ducked it. But I want to say one thing: We can be proud of it—5½ years. No man or no woman came into this Administration and left it with more of this world's goods than when he came in. No man or no woman ever profited at the public expense or the public till. That tells something about you.

Mistakes, yes. But for personal gain, never. You did what you believed in. Sometimes right, sometimes wrong. And I only wish that I were a wealthy man—at the present time, I have got to find a way to pay my taxes—[laughter]—and if I were, I would like to recompense you for the sacrifices that all of you have made to serve in government.

But you are getting something in government—and I want to tell this to your children, and I hope the Nation's children will hear it, too—something in government service that is far more important than money. It is a cause bigger than yourself. It is the cause of making this the greatest nation in the world, the leader of the world, because without our leadership, the world will know nothing but war, possibly starvation or worse, in the years ahead. With our leadership it will know peace, it will know plenty.

We have been generous, and we will be more generous in the future as we are able to. But most important, we must be strong here, strong in our hearts, strong in our souls, strong in our belief, and strong in our willingness to sacrifice, as you have been willing to sacrifice, in a pecuniary way, to serve in government.

There is something else I would like for you to tell your young people. You know, people often come in and say, 'What will I tell my kids?' They look at government and say, sort of a rugged life, and they see the mistakes that are made. They get the impression that everybody is here for the purpose of feathering his nest. That is why I made this earlier point—not in this Administration, not one single man or woman.

And I say to them, there are many fine careers. This country needs good farmers, good businessmen, good plumbers, good carpenters.

I remember my old man. I think that they would have called him sort of a little man, common man. He didn't consider himself that way. You know what he was? He was a streetcar motorman first, and then he was a farmer, and then he had a lemon ranch. It was the poorest lemon ranch in California, I can assure you. He sold it before they found oil on it. [Laughter] And then he was a grocer. But he was a great man, because he did his job, and every job counts up to the hilt, regardless of what happens.

Nobody will ever write a book, probably, about my mother. Well, I guess all of you would say this about your mother—my mother was a saint. And I think of her, two boys dying of tuberculosis, nursing four others in order that she could take care of my older brother for three years in Arizona, and seeing each of them die, and when they died, it was like one of her own.

Yes, she will have no books written about her. But she was a saint.

Now, however, we look to the future. I had a little quote in the speech last night from T. R. [Teddy Roosevelt]. As you know, I kind of like to read books. I am not educated, but I do read books—[laughter]—and the T. R. quote was a pretty good one.

Here is another one I found as I was reading, my last night in the White House, and this quote is about a young man. He was a young lawyer in New York. He had married a beautiful girl, and they had a lovely daughter, and then suddenly she died, and this is what he wrote. This was in his diary.

173

He said, "She was beautiful in face and form and lovelier still in spirit. As a flower she grew and as a fair young flower she died. Her life had been always in the sunshine. There had never come to her a single great sorrow. None ever knew her who did not love and revere her for her bright and sunny temper and her saintly unselfishness. Fair, pure and joyous as a maiden, loving, tender and happy as a young wife. When she had just become a mother, when her life seemed to be just begun and when the years seemed so bright before her, then by a strange and terrible fate death came to her. And when my heart's dearest died, the light went from my life forever."

That was T. R. in his 20s. He thought the light had gone from his life forever—but he went on. And he not only became President but, as an ex-President, he served his country, always in the arena, tempestuous, strong, sometimes wrong, sometimes right, but he was a man.

And as I leave, let me say, that is an example I think all of us should remember. We think sometimes when things happen that don't go the right way; we think that when you don't pass the bar exam the first time—I happened to, but I was just lucky; I mean, my writing was so poor the bar examiner said, "We have just got to let the guy through." We think that when someone dear to us dies, we think that when we lose an election, we think that when we suffer a defeat that all is ended. We think, as T. R. said, that the light had left his life forever.

Not true. It is only a beginning, always. The young must know it; the old must know it. It must always sustain us, because the greatness comes not when things go always good for you, but the greatness comes and you are really tested, when you take some knocks, some disappointments, when sadness comes, because only if you have been in the deepest valley can you ever know how magnificent it is to be on the highest mountain.

And so I say to you on this occasion, as we leave, we leave proud of the people who have stood by us and worked for us and served this country.

We want you to be proud of what you have done. We want you to continue to serve in government, if that is your wish. Always give your best, never get discouraged, never be petty; always remember, others may hate you, but those who hate you don't win unless you hate them, and then you destroy yourself.

And so, we leave with high hopes, in good spirit, and with deep humili-
ty, and with very much gratefulness in our hearts. I can only say to each and
every one of you, we come from many faiths, we pray perhaps to different
gods—but really the same God in a sense—but I want to say for each and
every one of you, not only will we always remember you, not only will we
always be grateful to you but always you will be in our hearts and you will be
in our prayers.

Thank you very much.

Source: Richard Nixon Library and Birthplace Foundation, http://www.nixonfoundation.
    org/Research_Center/1974_pdf_files/1974_0245.pdf

President Ford's Statement Pardoning Richard Nixon, and Nixon's Statement in Response

On September 8, 1974, President Gerald R. Ford granted a full pardon to former President Richard M. Nixon for all "offenses against the United States" during his presidency. One day later, Ford read a proclamation explaining the reasons for his decision. Here is the full text of Ford's statement:

Ladies and gentlemen, I have come to a decision which I felt I should tell you, and all my fellow citizens, as soon as I was certain in my own mind and conscience that it is the right thing to do.

I have learned already in this office that only the difficult decisions come to this desk. I must admit that many of them do not look at all the same as the hypothetical questions that I have answered freely and perhaps too fast on previous occasions. My customary policy is to try and get all the facts and to consider the opinions of my countrymen and to take counsel with my most valued friends. But these seldom agree, and in the end the decision is mine.

To procrastinate, to agonize, to wait for a more favorable turn of events that may never come, or more compelling external pressures that may as well be wrong as right, is itself a decision of sorts and a weak and potentially dangerous course for a President to follow.

I have promised to uphold the Constitution, to do what is right as God gives me to see the right, and to do the very best I can for America. I have asked your help and your prayers, not only when I became President, but many times since.

The Constitution is the supreme law of our land and it governs our actions as citizens. Only the laws of God, which govern our consciences, are superior to it. As we are a Nation under God, so I am sworn to uphold our laws with the help of God. And I have sought such guidance and searched my own conscience with special diligence to determine the right thing for me to do with respect to my predecessor in this place, Richard Nixon, and his loyal wife and family.

Theirs is an American tragedy in which we all have played a part. It can go on and on and on or someone must write "The End" to it. I have concluded that only I can do that. And if I can, I must.

There are no historic or legal precedents to which I can turn in this matter, none that precisely fit the circumstances of a private citizen who has resigned the Presidency of the United States. But it is common knowledge that serious allegations and accusations hang like a sword over our former President's head as he tries to reshape his life, a great part of which was spent in the service of this country and by the mandate of its people.

After years of bitter controversy and divisive national debate, I have been advised and compelled to conclude that many months and perhaps more years will have to pass before Richard Nixon could hope to obtain a fair trial by jury in any jurisdiction of the United States under governing decisions of the Supreme Court.

I deeply believe in equal justice for all Americans, whatever their station or former station. The law, whether human or divine, is no respector of persons but the law is a respector or reality. The facts as I see them are that a former President of the United States, instead of enjoying equal treatment with any other citizen accused of violating the law, would be cruelly and excessively penalized either in preserving the presumption of his innocence or in obtaining a speedy determination of his guilt in order to repay a legal debt to society.

During this long period of delay and potential litigation, ugly passions would again be aroused, our people would again be polarized in their opinions, and the credibility of our free institutions of government would again be challenged at home and abroad. In the end, the courts might well hold that Richard Nixon had been denied due process and the verdict of history would be even more inconclusive with respect to those charges arising out of the period of his Presidency of which I am presently aware.

But it is not the ultimate fate of Richard Nixon that most concerns me—though surely it troubles every decent and compassionate person. Rather my concern is the immediate future of this great country. In this I dare not depend upon my personal sympathy as a longtime friend of the former President nor my professional judgment as a lawyer. And I do not.

As President, my primary concern must always be the greatest good of all the people of the United States, whose servant I am.

As a man, my first consideration is to be true to my own convictions and my own conscience.

My conscience tells me clearly and certainly that I cannot prolong the bad dreams that continue to reopen a chapter that is closed. My conscience tells me that only I, as President, have the Constitutional power to firmly shut and seal this book. My conscience says it is my duty, not merely to proclaim domestic tranquility, but to use every means I have to ensure it.

I do believe that the buck stops here and that I cannot rely upon public opinion polls to tell me what is right. I do believe that right makes might, and that if I am wrong ten angels swearing I was right would make no difference. I do believe with all my heart and mind and spirit that I, not as President but as a humble servant of God, will receive justice without mercy if I fail to show mercy.

Finally, I feel that Richard Nixon and his loved ones have suffered enough, and will continue to suffer no matter what I do, no matter what we as a great and good Nation can do together to make his goal of peace come true.

Now, therefore, I, Gerald R. Ford, President of the United States, pursuant to the pardon power conferred upon me by Article II, Section 2, of the Constitution, have granted and by these presents do grant a full, free, and absolute pardon unto Richard Nixon for all offenses against the United States which he, Richard Nixon, has committed or may have committed or taken part in during the period from January 20, 1969, through August 9, 1974.

In response to Ford's pardon, Nixon issued the following statement:

I have been informed that President Ford has granted me a full and absolute pardon for any charges which might be brought against me for actions taken during the time I was president of the United States. In accepting this pardon, I hope that his compassionate act will contribute to lifting the burden of Watergate from our country.

Here in California, my perspective on Watergate is quite different than it was while I was embattled in the midst of the controversy, and while I was still subject to the unrelenting daily demands of the presidency itself.

Looking back on what is still in my mind a complex and confusing maze of events, decisions, pressures and personalities, one thing I can see clearly now is that I was wrong in not acting more decisively and more forthrightly in dealing with Watergate, particularly when it reached the stage of judicial proceedings and grew from a political scandal into a national tragedy.

No words can describe the depths of my regret and pain at the anguish my mistakes over Watergate have caused the nation and the presidency—a nation I so deeply love and an institution I so greatly respect.

I know many fair-minded people believe that my motivations and action in the Watergate affair were intentionally self-serving and illegal. I now understand how my own mistakes and misjudgments have contributed to that belief and seemed to support it. This burden is the heaviest one of all to bear. That the way I tried to deal with Watergate was the wrong way is a burden I shall bear for every day of the life that is left to me.

Sources: Gerald R. Ford Library and Museum, http://www.fordlibrarymuseum.gov/library/ speeches/740060.htm; Houston Chronicle Online, http://www.chron.com/content/ interactive/special/watergate/pardon,html#nixon

SOURCES FOR FURTHER STUDY

Genovese, Michael A. *The Watergate Crisis*. Westport, CT: Greenwood Press, 1999. This title for young adults provides a good overview of the Watergate scandal, including biographical profiles and excerpts of several Watergate tapes.

Kilian, Pamela. *What Was Watergate?* New York: St. Martin's Press, 1990. Intended for a grade school audience, this work provides considerable background on events leading up to Watergate, then addresses each stage of the crisis in chronological order.

Kutler, Stanley. *The Wars of Watergate: The Last Crisis of Richard Nixon*. New York: Knopf, 1990. This book is regarded by many historians as the single most authoritative work on the Watergate scandal. Making extensive use of Nixon archival materials, the book is richly detailed and places the scandal in historical context.

Nixon, Richard M. *RN: The Memoirs of Richard Nixon*. New York: Grosset & Dunlap, 1978. A highly readable autobiography penned by Nixon himself. The book covers everything from Nixon's early years in politics to his defense of his conduct during the Watergate affair.

Olson, Keith W. *Watergate: The Presidential Scandal that Shook America*. Lawrence: University Press of Kansas, 2003. A concise and insightful overview of the Watergate scandal, written in a more easily accessible manner than many other Watergate accounts.

Small, Melvin. *The Presidency of Richard Nixon*. Lawrence: University Press of Kansas, 1999. A fascinating portrait of Nixon's years in the White House, with appropriate focus on the Watergate scandal.

Strober, Gerald S., and Deborah Hart Strober, eds. *Nixon: An Oral History of His Presidency*. New York: HarperCollins, 1994. This work gathers together interviews from a wide array of political figures and journalists to weave an interesting account of Nixon's presidency. As with other overviews of the Nixon presidency, this work devotes a lot of attention to Watergate.

BIBLIOGRAPHY

Books and Periodicals

Ambrose, Stephen E. *Nixon: Ruin and Recovery: 1973-1990.* New York: Simon and Schuster, 1991.

Ball, Howard. "*United States v. Nixon* Re-Examined." Paper presented at the 1987 Nixon Conference, Hofstra University, Hempstead, New York.

Ben-Veniste, Richard. "Shadows of Nixon, Watergate Still Cross Our National Life." *Houston Chronicle,* June 13, 1997.

Berger, Raoul. *Executive Privilege: A Constitutional Myth.* Cambridge, MA: Cambridge University Press, 1974.

Bernstein, Carl, and Bob Woodward. *All the President's Men.* New York: Simon & Schuster, 1974.

Bernstein, Carl, and Bob Woodward. *The Final Days.* New York: Simon & Schuster, 1976.

Bradlee, Benjamin C. "Watergate: The Biggest Story—And the Most Intense Moment of Our Lives." *Washington Post,* June 14, 1992.

Brill, Steven. "Pressgate." *Brill's Content,* July-August 1998.

Cannon, James. *Time and Change: Gerald Ford's Appointment with History.* New York: HarperCollins, 1994.

Colony, Len, and Robert Gettlin. *Silent Coup: The Removal of a President.* New York: St. Martin's Press, 1991.

Congressional Quarterly. *Watergate: Chronology of a Crisis.* Washington, DC: Congressional Quarterly Press, 1975.

Craig, Bruce. "The Search for Deep Throat." *Perspectives online,* Summer, 2002, http://www.historians.org/perspectives/issues/2002/Summer/bcraig.cfm.

Daniel, Douglass K. "Best of Times and Worst of Times: Investigative Reporting in Post-Watergate America." In *The Big Chill: Investigative Reporting in the Current Media Environment.* Edited by Marilyn Greenwald and Joseph Bernt. Ames: Iowa State University Press, 2000.

Dash, Samuel. *Chief Counsel: Inside the Ervin Committee—The Untold Story of Watergate.* New York: Random House, 1976.

Dean, John. *Blind Ambition: The White House Years.* New York: Simon & Schuster, 1976.

Dean, John. *Lost Honor.* Los Angeles: Stratford Press, 1982.

Drew, Elizabeth. *Washington Journal: The Events of 1973-1974*. New York: Random House, 1975.

Ehrlichman, John. *Witness to Power: The Nixon Years*. New York: Simon & Schuster, 1982.

Emery, Fred. *Watergate: The Corruption of American Politics and the Fall of Richard Nixon*. New York: Times Books, 1994.

Ervin, Sam. *The Whole Truth*. New York: Random House, 1980.

Ford, Gerald. *A Time to Heal: The Autobiography of Gerald R. Ford*. New York: Harper & Row, 1979.

Friedman, Leon, and William F. Levantrosser, eds. *Watergate and Afterward: The Legacy of Richard M. Nixon*. Westport, CT: Greenwood, 1992.

Frost, David. *"I Gave Them a Sword": Behind the Scenes of the Nixon Interviews*. New York: William Morrow, 1978.

Garment, Leonard. *In Search of Deep Throat: The Greatest Political Mystery of Our Time*. New York: Basic Books, 2001.

Genovese, Michael A. *The Watergate Crisis*. Westport, CT: Greenwood, 1999.

Haig, Alexander M., Jr., with Charles McCarry. *Inner Circles: How America Changed the World*. New York: Warner, 1982.

Haldeman, H.R. *The Haldeman Diaries: Inside the Nixon White House*. New York: Putnam, 1994.

Haldeman, H.R. with Joseph DiMona. *The Ends of Power*. New York: New York Times Books, 1978.

Harward, Donald W., ed. *Crisis in Confidence: The Impact of Watergate*. Boston: Little, Brown, 1974.

Hoff, Joan. *Nixon Reconsidered*. New York: Basic, 1994.

Jaworski, Leon. *The Right and the Power: The Prosecution of Watergate*. New York: Reader's Digest Press, 1976.

Kilian, Pamela. *What Was Watergate?* New York: St. Martin's Press, 1990.

Kutler, Stanley, ed. *Abuse of Power: The New Nixon Tapes*. New York: Free Press, 1997.

Kutler, Stanley. *The Wars of Watergate: The Last Crisis of Richard Nixon*. New York: Knopf, 1990.

Kutler, Stanley, ed. *Watergate: The Fall of Richard M. Nixon*. St. James, NY: Brandywine Press, 1997.

Liddy, G. Gordon. *Will: The Autobiography of G. Gordon Liddy*. New York: St. Martin's Press, 1980.

Lukas, J. Anthony. *Nightmare: The Underside of the Nixon Years*. Rev. ed. New York: Penguin, 1988.

Magruder, Jeb Stuart. *An American Life: One Man's Road to Watergate*. New York: Atheneum, 1974.

McQuaid, Kim. *The Anxious Years: America in the Vietnam-Watergate Era*. New York: Basic Books, 1989.

Mondale, Walter. *The Accountability of Power: Toward a Responsible Presidency*. New York: David McKay, 1975.

Nixon, Richard M. *In the Arena: A Memoir of Victory, Defeat, and Renewal.* New York: Simon and Schuster, 1990.

Nixon, Richard M. *RN: The Memoirs of Richard Nixon.* New York: Grosset & Dunlap, 1978.

Olson, Keith W. *Watergate: The Presidential Scandal that Shook America.* Lawrence: University Press of Kansas, 2003.

Price, Raymond. "A President's Non-Resignation Address: The Watergate Words Never Spoken." *New York Times,* December 22, 1996.

Price, Raymond. *With Nixon.* New York: Viking, 1977.

Ravitch, Diane, and Chester Finn. *What Do Our 17-Year-Olds Know?* New York: Harper and Row, 1987.

Reeves, Richard. "Assessing Watergate 30 Years Later." *New York Times,* June 23, 2002.

Sabato, Larry. *Feeding Frenzy: How Attack Journalism Has Transformed American Politics.* New York: Free Press, 1991.

Safire, William. *Before the Fall: An Inside View of the Pre-Watergate White House.* Garden City, NY: Doubleday, 1975.

Schudson, Michael. *Watergate in American Memory: How We Remember, Forget, and Reconstruct the Past.* New York: Basic, 1992.

Sirica, John J. *To Set the Record Straight: The Break-In, the Tapes, the Conspirators, and the Pardon.* New York: Norton, 1979.

Small, Melvin. *The Presidency of Richard Nixon.* Lawrence: University Press of Kansas, 1999.

Strober, Gerald S., and Deborah Hart Strober, eds. *Nixon: An Oral History of His Presidency.* New York: HarperCollins, 1994.

Sussman, Barry. *The Great Coverup: Nixon and the Scandal of Watergate.* New York: Crowell, 1974.

White, Theodore H. *The Making of the President 1972.* New York: Atheneum, 1973.

Online

Dean, John. *Unmasking Deep Throat* (e-book), *Salon,* 2002. http://www.salon.com/deepthroat/index.html.

Houston Chronicle. "Watergate: The 25th Anniversary." http://www.chron.com/content/interactive/special/watergate

National Archives and Records Administration. "Nixon Presidential Materials." http://www.archives.gov/nixon/index.html

Richard Nixon Library and Birthplace. http://www.nixonfoundation.org

Washington Post Online. "Revisiting Watergate." http://www.washingtonpost.com/wp-srv/national/longterm/watergate

DVD and VHS

The Nixon Interviews with David Frost. 5 vols. VHS. Los Angeles, CA: Universal, 1992.

Watergate. 3 vols. VHS. New York: Discovery Communications (Discovery Channel), 1998.

PHOTO CREDITS

INDEX

(ill.) denotes illustration